AF600635

THE CATHOLIC UNIVERSITY OF AMERICA
CANON LAW STUDIES
No. 380

Free Admission to the Church for Sacred Rites

A DISSERTATION

Submitted to the Faculty of the School of Canon Law of The Catholic University of America in Partial Fulfillment of the Requirements for the Degree of Doctor of Canon Law

BY

REVEREND ALBERT C. ERNST, A.B., J.C.L.
Priest of the Diocese of Little Rock

THE CATHOLIC UNIVERSITY OF AMERICA PRESS
WASHINGTON, D. C.
1964

Free Admission to the Church for Sacred Rites

This dissertation was approved by the Right Reverend Monsignor Edward G. Roelker, S.T.D., J.C.D., Professor of Canon Law, as director, and by the Reverend Thomas O. Martin, Ph.D., S.T.D., J.C.D., LL.M., and the Reverend Romaeus W. O'Brien, O.Carm., M.A., J.C.D., as readers.

THE CATHOLIC UNIVERSITY OF AMERICA
CANON LAW STUDIES
No. 380

Free Admission to the Church for Sacred Rites

A DISSERTATION

Submitted to the Faculty of the School of Canon Law of The Catholic University of America in Partial Fulfillment of the Requirements for the Degree of Doctor of Canon Law

BY

REVEREND ALBERT C. ERNST, A.B., J.C.L.
Priest of the Diocese of Little Rock

THE CATHOLIC UNIVERSITY OF AMERICA PRESS
WASHINGTON, D. C.
1964

Nihil Obstat:

EDUARDUS ROELKER, S.T.D., J.C.D.
Censor Deputatus

Washingtonii, D. C., die 29 iunii, 1957

Imprimatur:

✠ ALBERTUS L. FLETCHER, D.D.
Episcopus Petriculanus

Petriculae, die 3 iulii, 1957

Printed by
THE WICKERSHAM PRINTING COMPANY
Lancaster, Pennsylvania

DEDICATED
IN HONOR OF MY
MOTHER AND FATHER
TO
THE IMMACULATE HEART OF MARY

FOREWORD

In most areas of the world, the Church looks for the acquittal of its temporal needs to the voluntary contributions of the faithful. That this obligation of the faithful to support the Church has its foundation in the natural law itself is not to be denied. Since the Church needs temporal means to fulfill its divine mission, it has an indisputable right to demand that those who benefit from its services will also provide the Church with the necessary help and aid.

In some countries indeed the State supplies the financial assistance required by the Church; but, by and large, in most countries the donations of the people themselves must provide the necessary wherewithal for the Church to carry out its purposes.

In the early days of Catholicism in the United States, the Church's needs were many and varied. But, inasmuch as the voluntary contributions of the faithful too often proved inadequate to meet those needs, other means had to be devised for supplementing the necessary income. The so-called Offertory collection, various family assessment plans, the payment of pew rent, and the collecting of seat money constitute but a few of the innovations that appeared in the course of time.

The parochial clergy of the United States has always been forced to struggle with the problem of inducing peoples of widely different nationalities and mentalities to practice their common religion and support it with some degree of harmony. Many of the early parishioners were immigrants from European nations, where the Church had been established for centuries. In such places the financial demands made upon them were considerably less than those of a missionary country such as this. Many therefore found it difficult to accept readily and conscientiously the greatly increased financial burden which suddenly confronted them. Added to this was the fact that most of these early congregations were largely composed of persons having, at best, an extremely modest income.

These and similar factors undoubtedly taxed the resourcefulness of pastors to a maximum degree. Theirs was the unenviable task of obtaining sufficient funds not only to provide for the ordinary pursuits of religion, but often to mold from the very foundations the material structure of the Church.

"It is not surprising, therefore, that all possible methods of raising funds were brought into play, and that occasionally, in sheer desperation, fantastic and even questionable schemes for increasing the revenues were resorted to." [1]

Probably the most widespread of all such "questionable schemes" is the one known as "door collections." Basically, this innovation is a practice whereby money is demanded or collected from the faithful at the door of the church as they enter to be present for divine services.

The Code of Canon Law makes the following demand:

> Admission to the church for sacred rites must be absolutely free of charge, all contrary custom being reprobated.[2]

Collections taken up at the church door, therefore, are in direct violation of this ecclesiastical prohibition. In addition, since the law itself expressly repudiates all contrary customs, not even those of immemorial duration may be tolerated.

The purpose of this dissertation, then, encompasses the scope and ramifications of canon 1181. In pursuit of its end, it purports to trace the development, in the United States, of the aforementioned practice, and to enumerate some of the more common abuses of this nature.

Only briefly does it deal with the application of the canon to the practices of other countries. It likewise is not concerned directly with the payment of pew rent or so-called seat money, both of which are lawful means of revenue. Occasionally, how-

[1] Kremer, *Church Support in the United States*, The Catholic University of America Canon Law Studies, No. 61 (Washington, D. C.: The Catholic University of America, 1930), p. 68.

[2] "Ingressus in ecclesiam ad sacros ritus sit omnino gratuitus, reprobata qualibet contraria consuetudine."—*Codex Iuris Canonici Pii X Maximi iussu digestus Benedicti Papae XV auctoritate promulgatus* (Romae: Typis Polyglottis Vaticanis, 1917), canon 1181. Hereinafter simply the canon will be cited.

ever, the methods used to obtain such otherwise legitimate income must be denounced when they run contrary to the prohibitions of ecclesiastical law.

Finally, an effort will be made to sketch the background and consequence of the many condemnations, both general and particular, which demand that all such practices and abuses, in whatsoever manner they exist, be universally abolished.

The writer gladly welcomes this occasion for expressing a profound gratitude to His Excellency, the Most Reverend Albert L. Fletcher, D.D., Bishop of Little Rock, for providing the opportunity to do graduate studies in the School of Canon Law at the Catholic University of America, and for affording the generosity without which this publication would not have been possible. He wishes to thank, also, the Right Reverend Monsignor James E. O'Connell, Rector of St. John's Seminary, Little Rock, Arkansas, the Right Reverend Monsignor Joseph A. Murray, Chancellor of the Diocese, and the Very Reverend Monsignor Lawrence P. Graves, J.C.L., *Officialis,* for their many kindnesses, in the form of assistance, encouragement, and suggestions, during the preparation of this work and throughout the three years of advanced study.

Likewise, to the Faculty of the School of Canon Law for their invaluable instruction and guidance, to the Readers of the dissertation for their helpful suggestions, and to his classmates and fellow priests for the inspiration and assistance which they provided on so many occasions, the author is extremely grateful.

A note of thanks is also extended to the Most Reverend Bishops and Chancellors, in the United States and elsewhere, who generously gave of their time to respond to an archdiocesan and diocesan survey of local custom and practice which the writer conducted in the course of preparing the dissertation. Their comments and suggestions have been most helpful.

Last, but not least, he wishes to thank his mother and father, his sister and brother and their families, and all others who helped in any way, and whose prayers and encouragement are in no small way responsible for this publication.

TABLE OF CONTENTS

CHAPTER I

METHODS EMPLOYED IN COLLECTING MONEY FROM THE FAITHFUL AT THE CHURCH DOORS

Prior to any consideration of the various laws which demand free admission to the church for sacred rites, it seems proper to acquaint the reader with a few of the practices themselves which led to such legislation, and to examine other abuses of a similar nature which have sprung up from time to time, even after ecclesiastical condemnation. The variety of these practices seems to be limited only by the measure of ingenuity on the part of the pastors responsible for their instigation. Some of the methods employed in collecting money at the church door are quite simple and unpretentious, while others assume the air of a well-organized, efficient, thriving business enterprise. Needless to say, some of these methods continue today, despite the specific repudiation of all such abuses.

It is readily understandable that persons who are engaged in violating the law hesitate to publish books elaborating on their methods of infraction. Since, however, these practices, sad to say, are fairly widespread, one needs little more than an adventuresome spirit in order to view firsthand the *modus operandi* of the modern day money changer in the temple. If, happily, gratuitous access to sacred rites is accorded to all in one's own domicile, he has but to travel perhaps no farther than to a neighboring diocese, to a popular resort area, or to some of our country's larger cities to discover that at least in some churches of the locality a collection is taken up at the door. Investigation has shown that no section of the country is completely without fault on this score. Fairness, however, dictates mention of the fact that in certain areas and in many dioceses door collections are entirely unknown, or at least extremely rare, though in other places they are rather common.

Many of the practices treated below have been observed by the writer personally; others came to his attention by way of ninety-nine generous replies received in response to a survey of most of this country's archdiocesan and diocesan chanceries, relative to the subject matter in question; and a few were brought to light through discussions with other priests in the course of preparing the present dissertation. The reader is to be assured that no attempt is made to overemphasize any of the abuses described herein, to add any undue stress, or to substitute imagination for reality. Undoubtedly, however, many will be surprised to learn that practices so unreasonable as some of those which await mention could ever gain force.

Perhaps the most common method of violating the law is that which allows ushers or other laymen to stand at the church doors with baskets, boxes, or similar implements to receive the voluntary donations of the people as they enter the house of God for divine services. No effort is made to demand a set fee from anyone, but each adult is expected to make *some* offering as he enters. Though seemingly innocent, such a practice is nonetheless forbidden. As will be pointed out later, the Sacred Congregation for the Propagation of the Faith viewed such an innovation with alarm, and feared that it might exert undue moral pressure against some of the faithful, particularly the poor, by causing them to remain away from sacred functions rather than to suffer the embarrassment of passing the collectors without being able to contribute the expected offering. In 1862, the Fathers of the III Provincial Council of Cincinnati were notified that Pope Pius IX expressed his personal displeasure upon hearing that such a practice existed in three cities of the Diocese of Cleveland. Even though no one was actually prevented from hearing Mass if he could not make an offering, the Supreme Pontiff demanded that the innovation be stopped within two years.

Slightly more aggressive is a method in which the ushers, instead of being merely passive, let it be known to all those who enter the church that they are expected to contribute a specified amount, usually ten or twenty-five cents. And, with a little experience, ushers generally become extremely proficient at campaigning for this entrance fee. They take their jobs very seriously and feel that theirs is an obligation, a sort of sacred trust, to see to it that only children and the notably poor adults are allowed to enter "free of charge." Often, even these latter are reluctantly permitted to pass only when it becomes evident that further persuasion would be futile or would cause great embarrassment. These ushers are, for the most part, in good faith, and they can not be held personally responsible for their lack of knowledge concerning the Code of Canon Law. They receive their instructions from the pastor and seek simply to carry out his wishes, believing implicitly, and probably without any positive advertence to the fact, that he would not direct them to do anything contrary to Church law.

In variations of the foregoing practices the ushers stand, not at the church doors themselves, but just inside the doors or in the vestibule, in order to accept the "offerings" of the faithful as they enter the church. This escape mechanism was devised at an early date to circumvent the wording of the Plenary Councils of Baltimore which forbade the exacting of money "*at the doors* of churches." Adherents to this erroneous interpretation refuse to accept the *entire* context of the Baltimore prohibition, and they fail to appreciate how the foresight of the Fathers of the II Plenary Council (and probably their understanding of human nature) actually led to a change in the wording of the decree in question for the specific purpose of condemning *all* such contrary abuses.[1]

Moreover, in a special Admonition, dated August 15, 1869, the Sacred Congregation for the Propagation of the Faith expressed its awareness of this method of subterfuge and demanded its suppression.[2]

In some churches there are placed at the doors, or at the entrances to the various aisles, money stands for the "convenience" of the faithful. These stands contain an opening, or slot, into which coins may be deposited by the people as they pass. The money thus received drops into a box (which has been previously inserted and securely locked within the stand itself)

[1] Cf. *infra,* pp. 48-49. After deliberation, the decree was changed to read, in effect: "The practice of demanding money at the doors of churches, wherever and *in whatever way it exists* . . . is to be abolished."

[2] Cf. *infra,* pp. 52-54.

where it remains until all the boxes are collected and emptied for counting—generally after eaeh Mass. The stands frequently are attended by ushers, and they usually display a sign indicating that each adult is expected to deposit ten or twenty-five cents, etc.

Needless to say, this practice is no less offensive than those previously described, and it is to be condemned with equal severity.

The most outrageous attack against the doctrine of free admission to sacred functions is the shameful abuse perpetrated by the actual erection of turnstiles at the entrances to the church or to the aisles thereof. These turnstiles bear a marked resemblance to those which are to be found in such places as subways and athletic stadiums, and they are undoubtedly installed for the similar purpose of rendering more expeditious the collection of a compulsory entrance fee from all comers. Their existence, at least in the recent past, has been verified in no less than five different cities. Such an abomination needs no specific arguments to point out its dangers, and it should not be dignified even to the extent of simply listing the various objections to its existence. Even were door collections allowed by the law, the scandal which would certainly be caused by the obnoxious presence of turnstiles would thereby render them absolutely and completely condemned.

Another popular abuse, but of a somewhat different nature, is that in which a table or booth is set up in the church vestibule for the purpose of changing money (if necessary) and accepting the "customary" entrance fee. The number of such tables will vary with the size of the church, but each is staffed with one or more laymen (ushers, wardens, etc.) who supervise the making of change and the actual collection of the tax.

Usually the tables are very simple and unpretentious. But quite often, particularly in large parishes, they assume overwhelmingly elaborate proportions. Some are specially constructed of decorative woods; many are enclosed at the bottom and faced with glass on the upper part of the front and sides. In general, they resemble in many ways the typical theatre ticket booth.

When this system is employed, a set fee is anticipated from each adult, and the attendants usually refuse to accept more than the expected amount. If more is offered by any individual, strangely enough he is generally given change.

This basic type of table or booth is widely used throughout the country in places where entrance fees are in vogue. The manner, however, in which the table is utilized, and its relation to the overall system employed by any particular church for collecting entrance fees, differs from place to place.

In its simplest form, there is practiced in many parishes what could be called the "honor system." Only one money table is located in the vestibule, and all the parishioners are expected to stop and make the customary contribution. If, however, some of them so choose, they are free to ignore the collectors and proceed, unmolested, into the church.

In a slightly modified version of this method, the lone money table is indeed found duly attended in the vestibule, but additional ushers or other laymen are stationed at the aisle entrances to observe that all make the customary stop at the table before taking a seat in the church. Occasionally strangers unknowingly overlook the collection table; they are courteously reminded of its presence by the ushers. Others are sometimes "bold enough" to ignore the system *deliberately*. Their chances of escape are not too good. Over-zealous ushers have not been unknown to pursue such "gate crashers" down the aisle in order to retrieve the entrance fee, thereby creating much embarrassment, ill will, and even scandal.

Human respect, an antipathy for non-conformity, abhorrence for conspicuousness, and a fear of embarrassment are but a few of the reasons whereby many, who otherwise are opposed to door collections, are coerced into paying the fee rather than "bucking" the system or challenging the usher who "guards" the aisle.

Evidently striving for greater efficiency, someone conceived the idea of roping off the church aisles and selling tickets at the vestibule tables. The resultant system was thereby rendered practically foolproof, in that it reduced to a scientific minimum the task of the usher. He was no longer challenged to a proverbial battle of wits by the occasional non-conformist who repeatedly dodged the money tables. Nor was he temporarily immobilized whenever a large crowd—possibly containing a gate crasher or two—converged at one of the aisle entrances. Now, the presence of the rope allowed the usher to control the rate of entry; and the resultant procedure was reduced simply to establishing a count and collecting an equal number of tickets.

The method of obtaining revenue through the sale of tickets for admission to divine services was probably introduced about the middle of the last century, along with some of the other innovations described above. As early as 1869, in the *Acta* of the II Provincial Council of Australia, there was mention of such a practice. Needless to say, it was immediately condemned by the Holy See.[3]

In the United States this practice of purchasing tickets probably began in connection with the celebration of Masses on the great Feasts of Christmas and Easter. Later it was adopted in some places on a week to week basis. Although the sale of tickets for attendance at services on big feasts seems to have been quite popular for a time (and indeed it is still in vogue in some areas), the use of such tickets on Sundays and holy days, while prevalent in many places (even today), was in no sense quite as widespread.

In a circular letter to the bishops of the United States, dated September 29, 1911, the Apostolic Delegate wrote: "It was said that in some localities tickets for entrance to the church . . . were previously sold, and especially on the occasion of Christmas, Easter, etc., and were then demanded at the door of the church." The letter emphatically adds: ". . . there is here a question of a practice really reprehensible and already condemned. . . . It has long been known to all how strongly the Holy See has reprobated all practices of this kind, their explicit condemnation having been made by Pius IX in the year 1862."[4]

The results of a survey, made in 1956, of some of the principal metropolitan sees throughout Europe indicate that there have been occasional problems connected with ticket selling, principally for the Midnight Mass of Christmas, in some of those countries also.

[3] Cf. *infra*, pp. 89-90.

[4] Cf. *infra*, pp. 86-87.

One questionable practice is that in which money changing tables are located in the vestibule, but not for the purpose of accepting an entrance fee. In many churches "seat money" is collected from the parishioners after they enter the pews or during divine services. This is perhaps not the most desirable means of obtaining revenue, but it is not forbidden by canon law. One great disadvantage of such a collection, however, lies in the fact that only ten or twenty-five cents is accepted from each adult, and many will not always have the exact amount ready. This necessitates the making of change and a double transfer of money between parishioner and usher. All of this adds up to distraction and even confusion. In an effort to eliminate much of the undesirableness of such a system, some churches have installed money tables in the vestibule for the sole purpose of providing the people with correct change as they enter, and thereby facilitating the seat money collections which will later be taken up during divine services.

Many places have transferred the seat money collection itself from the body of the church to the vestibule, where it is taken up as the people enter for Mass. This is forbidden directly by the law, which, although it allows seat money to be collected, forbids that it be taken up at the entrance to the church.

To have a table in the vestibule solely for the purpose of making change does not seem to violate inherently (*per se*) the directives of the general law or of the Councils of Baltimore. It is, however, unwise to institute such an operation. One of the reasons for prohibiting money-collections at the door is the scandal that is thus occasioned for the faithful. The very fact of a coin table near the entrance of the church, and the making of change there, gives the impression that money is being collected. Also, the close association of this practice with repudiated abuses is all the more reason for its not being permitted. It is best to have the entranceway free of anything that even vaguely resembles a collector's stand. In this manner, not only the letter but also the spirit of the law is completely fulfilled.

As a final item, the writer wishes to make mention of an unusual practice which was brought to his attention in the course of his preparation of the present dissertation. It is an extremely novel approach to the problem of church support, and, in so far as is known, has existed in only one place in the United States. The ingenuity and inventive genius of the pastor who conceived the system are worthy of note, despite the fact that his plan, as will be evident, may hardly be tolerated.

The parish in question boasted of only a moderate number of steadily residing parishioners. Being, however, located near a large resort area, its ranks were swelled "in season" by the influx of visitors. The pastor apparently had the good will of the generally "well-to-do tourists" in the area, and his unique and humorous idea for encouraging their financial assistance operated in the form of a door collection. Each week an announcement was made in church to the effect that next Sunday would be, for example, "license plate Sunday." The following week as each person entered the church he was requested to give his license plate number. He was then asked by one of the ushers for a contribution equivalent in amount to the first three figures of that number. Thus, if the license plate read: 156-279, a donation of one dollar and fifty-six cents was sought.

The following Sunday might be designated "scale Sunday." On that day, several scales would be placed in the vestibule so that each person, as he entered the church, could "weigh in" to determine the size of his contribution. Someone weighing one hundred and seventy-five pounds, for example, was expected to donate one dollar and seventy-five cents, etc. This latter procedure was probably not too popular with the ladies; it is reported, however, that financially the system was a "terrific success." It is apparent that variations of the method are limited only by the extent of the imagination. Needless to say, the errors of such a practice are so self-evident that no further discussion or elaboration seems necessary.

Lastly, it should be noted that many diocesan statutes promulgate for their respective territories particular laws which regulate money-collecting in accord with the circumstances of the area. Some of these forbid the presence of any money tables whatsoever in the vestibule of the church; others outlaw the collecting of seat money altogether, and so forth. These statutes will be treated in a later part of the present work.

CHAPTER II

SIMONY AND DOOR COLLECTIONS

Almost from its very inception has the Church been plagued with numerous practices and schemes instigated for the sole purpose of buying and selling various spiritual things. Such abuses have come to be known under the general heading of simony, taking their name from one Simon Magus who, as the Scriptures tell us, sought to purchase the power of the Holy Ghost from the Apostles and was soundly rebuked by St. Peter.[1] Although similar practices existed even in pre-Christian times, the growth and complexity of the Church, together with the rapid spread of Christianity, provided many fertile fields for the germination of these seeds of sacrilege.

St. Thomas Aquinas (1225-1274) appropriated the description of simony given by many of the early glossators when he defined it as "a deliberate design of selling or buying, for a temporal price, such things as are spiritual or annexed unto spirituals."[2]

The Code of Canon Law, in its treatment of the subject, adopts the basic definition of St. Thomas and augments it with the inclusion of various other qualifying notes:

> The deliberate will to buy or sell for a temporal price things intrinsically spiritual, e.g. the Sacraments, ecclesiastical jurisdiction, consecration, indulgences, etc., or to buy or sell a temporal thing annexed to a spiritual thing in such a way that the temporal thing cannot exist independently, e.g. an ecclesiastical benefice, etc., or to make the spiritual thing even the partial object of a contract, e.g. the consecration in the sale of a consecrated chalice, is simony forbidden by the divine law.
>
> To give temporal things annexed to spirituals for other

[1] Acts, VIII:14-24.

[2] "Studiosa voluntas emendi vel vendendi aliquid spirituale, et spirituali annexum [pro pretio temporali]."—St. Thomas Aquinas, *Summa Theologica* (4 vols., Taurini: Marietti, 1948), IIa IIae, q. 100, a. 1.

> temporal things annexed to spirituals, or spirituals for spirituals, or even temporal things for temporal things, if it is forbidden by the Church on account of the danger or irreverence to spiritual things, is simony forbidden by ecclesiastical law.[3]

It is evident that through simony the delinquent undertakes, deliberately, to equalize the spiritual and the temporal. In a sense, he intends to commercialize something spiritual by demanding or exacting a charge for its use, reception or conferral. It is specifically this problem which plagued the Church time and again, especially in the earlier centuries of the Middle Ages. Yet the close connection between the natural and the supernatural order, and the obvious difficulties connected with drawing a line of demarcation between the two, particularly in the earlier days, led to added conflicts and greatly involved remedies.

Because of its obvious horror of the abuse in any form, the Church passed very stringent laws and meted out severe penalties in all things pertaining to simony. The Church was especially severe with all those who were involved in simoniacal practices pertaining to the Mass, the Sacraments, Orders and the Episcopacy. Moreover, even those things which contained the appearance of simony were to be shunned at all costs. Numerous and minute distinctions were utilized whenever there was a question of exacting, requesting, or contracting by pact for a temporal payment in return for some spiritual benefit, or even for those temporal things which were intimately connected with the spiritual.

One such abuse in the Church's history was occasioned by the advent of monasticism. Many viewed the religious life as a means of securing an easy livelihood. All too often, particularly if the monastery was not well endowed, unscrupulous Religious saw in the holy desire of man to embrace the religious state a chance for self-aggrandizement. Simony in admission to the religious state became a problem, and the usual plea in defense of the abuse was the poverty of the monastery.[4]

[3] Can. 727, § 1, § 2.

[4] Ryder, *Simony, An Historical Synopsis and Commentary,* The Catholic University of America Canon Law Studies, No. 65 (Washington, D. C.: The Catholic University of America, 1931), pp. 29-30.

In the *Decretum* of Gratian (c. 1140) this practice was treated at great length. Typical is the following text:

> Whence it is easily seen that those about to enter a monastery should offer their goods to the ruling superiors, and should be received only after they have offered their goods. But it is one thing to offer one's goods of one's own accord; it is another to pay what has been exacted. . . . Therefore, it is not permitted . . . that ruling superiors exact anything from those who enter, but they may take what has been offered freely, because the former is worthy of condemnation, but the latter in no wise so.[5]

Commenting on this Second Question of Gratian in reference to entrance to a monastery, Rolandus Bandinelli, later Pope Alexander III, pointed out the following in his *Summa* (c. 1150):

> The Second Question is whether money is to be exacted for entrance to the church, etc. Regarding this, it is to be noted that of those things which are offered, some are given voluntarily, others under compulsion; at the same time, some are given by reason of an agreement, others through mere liberality. However, nothing is to be exacted out of compulsion or by agreement for the reception of a sacred thing. Therefore, nothing is to be exacted for entrance into the church. For this reason, nothing whatsoever is to be exacted, or if exacted, is to be paid; nor is anything to be asked by agreement for entrance to the church."[6]

This distinction between what was offered out of liberality and what was exacted in the form of a payment for a spiritual thing was thus early insisted upon by the canonical authors. It continued as the basis for the difference between simoniacal handling of sacred things and the generous return from the faithful out of gratitude for spiritual benefits brought to them by the ministers of God.

Other practices, such as the purchasing of benefices, the charging of a fee for performing spiritual functions, and the demanding of a payment for ordination were equally condemned.

Throughout their expositions on the matter of simony, the

[5] *Corpus Iuris Canonici* (2. ed., 2 vols., Richter-Friedberg, Leipzig, 1922), I Pars, § 2, ante c. 1, C. I, q. 2.

[6] *Summa Magistri Rolandi* (ed. Thaner, Innsbruck, 1874), ad c. 1, C. I, q. 2.

authors point out that those things are not simoniacal in which a temporal price is attached to the external circumstances connected with various spiritual functions. Thus, for example, those who have the duty of the sacred ministry are severely warned and commanded that they are freely to give what they have freely received. Yet, without engaging in any form of business, such ministers of God must obtain a livelihood. For this reason the priest and other sacred ministers may accept and retain what is voluntarily offered for their support. The priest may also, without reference to any pact, price, or exaction, receive recompense for those activities which are connected with his work in such a manner that they are not intimately joined with the spiritual ministrations which are his duty, so that paying for one would likewise constitute paying for the other.

It is thus that one may consider the practice—existing in some areas—of demanding money from the faithful at the door of the church as they enter to be present for the Holy Sacrifice of the Mass or for other sacred functions. It is a practice which, outwardly, resembles the abuse of simony. One may safely say that in places where door collections are taken up there is no intent to charge, simoniacally, for the privilege of attending the sacred mysteries. Nevertheless, the effect produced is extremely similar. When a stranger is confronted for the first time with such a practice, the result quite generally is a natural one. Though he may know nothing about Canon Law, almost intuitively his intellect informs him that he should not have to pay to attend Mass. Prescinding from the spiritual treasures of the Holy Sacrifice, he reasons, first, that the Church demands his presence on Sundays and holy days unless he be legitimately excused of dispensed and, secondly, that when he presents himself in fulfillment of this obligation, he must pay to enter. The "Church," he feels, is taking unfair advantage of him.

Those who employ this method of collecting present various arguments in defense of their action. Basically, they contend that the money thus obtained is not a payment for admission, and that, on the contrary, such a system provides a means whereby all the parishioners may share, more or less equally, the burden of providing for the necessary parochial expenses.

In view of what has gone before, it can be concluded that only this fact, namely that the temporal price is attached to some *external circumstances* connected with spiritual functions, saves the abuse of "demanding money from the faithful at the door of the church" from the nature and penalties of simony.

Nevertheless, what the authors have to say about simony may be appropriated by way of analogy to this offensive practice. Though not simoniacal in itself, it is so intimately connected with the spiritual function of attending sacred services in the church, that it has been condemned and repudiated by positive legislation. Thus an attempt is made to eliminate even the appearance of simony, to remove a possible source of scandal to the faithful, and to protect the Church itself from any ill-repute, unwarranted criticism, or unjust imputation.

CHAPTER III

DEFINITION OF TERMS

Prior to any detailed consideration of the scope of canon 1181, it is necessary to establish a few norms relative to the terms used in the canon itself. The law, as enacted in the Code, stresses three elements: a) free admission, b) to the church, c) for sacred rites. Primary emphasis is undoubtedly placed upon gratuitous access *to the sacred rites* themselves. In the following exposition, therefore, this latter component will be given first consideration.

Article 1. Sacred Rites

Basic to a definition of sacred rites is an agreement as to the meaning of the term "rite." The word itself, as used by authors, has a variety of applications. Fundamentally, Webster defines it as "a prescribed form or manner of conducting a ceremony, esp. a religious ceremony; . . . a ritual for a religious service."[1]

A somewhat more elaborate description is the following:

> In English the word "rite" ordinarily means the ceremonies, prayers, and functions of any religious body whether pagan, Jewish, Moslem, or Christian. But here we must distinguish two uses of the word. We speak of any one such religious function as a rite—the rite of the blessing of palms, the coronation rite, etc. In a slightly different sense we call the whole complex of the services of any Church or group of Churches a rite.[2]

This provides a substantial, if not a comprehensive, criterion from which to proceed. Although the word itself may be employed in a more generic sense, it usually connotes something religious; and frequently it is associated with the term "ceremonies," as in the expression "rites and ceremonies." The in-

[1] *Webster's New International Dictionary of the English Language* (William A. Neilson, Editor in chief, 3 vols., 2. ed., Springfield, Mass.: G. & C. Merriam Co., 1953).

[2] *The Catholic Encyclopedia* (15 vols. and 2 supplements, New York: Robert Appleton Co., 1907-1922), XIII, 64.

discriminate use of these two terms and the variety of subjective distinctions between them, as put forth by many authors, lead to much confusion.

Some hold that by "ceremonies" one is to understand the sacred actions themselves which are performed in acts of worship, and by "rites," the manner in which these actions are carried out; others hold that the rites are the substantial and profound arrangement or order to be found in divine worship, whereas the ceremonies are in great part accidental and secondary. Some view the rites as the prayers used in various functions, and the ceremonies as the gestures or other bodily movements which accompany the prayers; and still others argue that rites and ceremonies signify one and the same thing, and hence may be used together or interchangeably.

Cappello speaks of a ceremony as being a sacred action, whereas "rite," having a three-fold distinction, denotes either a universal discipline, a peculiar system of liturgical laws, or (for the purpose here at hand) the order to be observed in the performing of a given function and the norms regulating the administration of each and every such function. Thus he writes:

> Vox *ritus* sumitur triplici sensu: *stricto, lato,* et *latissimo.* Sensu *stricto* denotat universam disciplinam late sumptam, ita ut complectatur etiam praescripta liturgica . . . ; sensu *lato* comprehendit peculiare legum praesertim liturgicarum systema . . . ; sensu *latissimo* significat ordinem administrationis seu complexum normarum, imo et singulas normas. *Caeremonia* generatim denotat ipsam sacram actionem.[3]

It is the opinion of Cappello that there should be a definite distinction between rites and ceremonies, although he admits that the terms are frequently used interchangeably.[4]

Van der Stappen († 1906)[5] and Coronata[6] regarded rites as

[3] Cappello, *Tractatus Canonico-Moralis De Sacramentis* (5 vols., Vol. I, 6. ed., Taurini: Marietti, 1953), I, n. 50.

[4] Cappello, *loc. cit.*

[5] Van der Stappen, *Sacra Liturgia* (3. ed., 5 vols., Mechliniae: H. Dessain, 1911-1915), I, n. 3.

[6] Coronata, *Institutiones Iuris Canonici* (5 vols., Vol. I, *Normae Generales, De Clericis, De Religiosis, De Laicis,* editio quarta, Taurini: Marietti, 1950), I, n. 1, p. 3 (hereafter cited *Institutiones*).

designating the prayers which are recited in the Mass, in the Divine Office, and in the administration of the Sacraments. The ceremonies, on the other hand, are the acts, gestures, and other bodily movements used in connection with the words or prayers. Van der Stappen, moreover, asserted that "ceremonies" include the things themselves, such as candles, incense, or vestments, over which or with which words or prayers are pronounced.[7]

Wernz (1842-1914)-Vidal (1867-1938), in treating this matter, wrote the following:

> Quo sensu restricto *caeremoniae* saepe opponuntur *ritibus* (sacris formulis *verborum, substantialibus* ritibus sacrificii et sacramentorum *a Christo* institutis) atque solummodo significant *gestus corporis* (actiones symbolicas, formas *accidentales*) *ab Ecclesia* in cultu divino institutas et additas.[8]

The Council of Trent spoke of a rite as being any lawfully prescribed method of externally performing sacred functions, while it referred to ceremonies as the exterior forms of divine worship, such as things or actions, ordered by the Church, and which have some symbolic spiritual significance or meaning.[9]

Michiels holds that the word "rite," in its proper sense, signifies the order or procedure set down by the Church for the performance of sacred functions: "Ritus ergo, proprio sensu, idem significat ac vocabulum 'ordo'. . . ."[10]

Significant also is the summary given by Michiels:

> Utendo verbis "ritus et caeremoniae," Codificator evidenter intendit omnes rubricas seu regulas, quae continent ritus et caeremonias, normas scilicet quae indicant quando et quomodo et quaenam preces dicendae sint, quinam ritus servandi in functionibus sacris peragendis.[11]

[7] Van der Stappen, *loc. cit.*

[8] Wernz-Vidal, *Ius Canonicum ad Codicis Normam Exactum* (7 vols. in 8, Vol. IV, *De Rebus,* Pars I, Romae: Apud Aedes Universitatis Gregorianae, 1934), IV, n. 410.

[9] Conc. Trident., sess. XXII, *de sacrificio missae,* c. 5.

[10] Michiels, *Normae Generales Juris Canonici* (2 vols., editio altera, Tornaci: Typis Societatis S. Joannis Evangelistae, Desclée et Socii, 1949), I, 58 (hereafter cited *Normae Generales*).

[11] *Loc. cit.*

Vermeersch (1858-1936)-Creusen concur in the opinion of Michiels, and add the fact that the word "rites" may be used in a generic sense to include also "ceremonies"; but the reverse is not true.[12]

From this it can be said, then, that in the liturgy a ceremony is an external gesture, action, or movement which accompanies the prayers and public exercise of divine worship; the sum total of all the ceremonies pertaining to a given function, plus the prayers or words prescribed for its performance, may be called a rite; and all the rites of a particular religion, when taken together, constitute its cult.

With this in mind, one may next seek to demonstrate what exactly is meant by *sacred* rites in the specific sense in which the term is applicable to the work at hand.

McManus states that a sacred rite is "the complexus and order of ceremonies, an entire function of worship." [13] This usage appears to have the sanction of ecclesiastical law, which tends to generalize its references to sacred rites in such a manner that the term becomes synonymous with the liturgy itself. And, as Oppenheim (1899-1949) reasoned, sacred rites and ceremonies embrace the interior and exterior acts of worship which are offered to God by the Church, through the medium of certain designated ministers, and with the participation of the faithful.[14]

> A Christian rite . . . comprises the manner of performing all services for the worship of God and the sanctification of men. This includes therefore: (1) the administration of sacraments, among which the service of the Holy Eucharist, as being also the Sacrifice, is the most important element of all; (2) the series of psalms, lessons, prayers, etc., divided into separate unities, called "hours," to make up together the Divine Office; (3) all other religious and ecclesiastical functions, called sacramentals. This general term includes

12 "Plura etiam quam caeremoniae ritus amplectitur. Namque uno *ritus* nomine etiam caeremonias, non autem uno *caeremoniarum* nomine etiam ritum appellaveris."—Vermeersch-Creusen, *Epitome Iuris Canonici* (3 vols., Vol. I, editio septima, Mechliniae: H. Dessain, 1949), I, n. 70 (hereafter cited *Epitome*).

13 McManus, *The Congregation of Sacred Rites,* The Catholic University of America Canon Law Studies, No. 352 (Washington, D. C.: The Catholic University of America Press, 1954), p. 5.

14 Oppenheim, *Institutiones Systematico-Historicae in Sacram Liturgiam,* Series I (6 vols., Taurini: Marietti, 1937-1941), VI, 40.

> blessings of persons (such as a coronation, the blessing of an abbot, various ceremonies performed for catechumens, the reconciliation of public penitents, Benediction of the Blessed Sacrament, etc.), blessings of things (the consecration of a church, altar, chalice, etc.), and a number of devotions and ceremonies, e.g. processions and the taking of vows. Sacraments, the Divine Office, and sacramentals (in a wide sense) make up the rite of any Christian religious body.[15]

The Congregation of Sacred Rites, which was created by Pope Sixtus V in 1588, has always listed among its functions the vigilance for the proper observance of the sacred rites. In the papal bull *Immensa aeterni Dei* of January 22, 1588, the Holy Father listed his reasons for establishing this Congregation. In so doing, he made this statement: "The Church, taught by the Holy Spirit and by Apostolic tradition and discipline, uses sacred rites and ceremonies in the administration of the sacraments, the divine offices, and the whole worship of God and the Saints." [16]

Pope St. Pius X (1903-1914) reiterated the duties of the Congregation of Sacred Rites and charged it to be vigilant for the proper observance of the sacred rites in the celebration of Mass, in the administration of the sacraments, in the performance of the Divine Office, and indeed in all that pertains to worship in the Latin Church.[17]

The Code states that the Congregation of Sacred Rites has authority to supervise and regulate all matters pertaining directly to the sacred rites and ceremonies of the Latin Church.[18]

In view of the foregoing, it may be said that these sacred rites embrace the entire order of services and functions which make up the liturgy. These services and functions may be enumerated as the Mass, the Sacraments, the Divine Office, and the special

[15] *The Catholic Encyclopedia,* XIII, 64.

[16] *Bullarum Diplomatum et Privilegiorum Romanorum Pontificum Taurinensis Editio* (24 vols. and Appendix, Augustae Taurinorum, 1857-1872), VIII, 989.

[17] Pius X, const. *Sapienti consilio,* 29 iun. 1908, § 1, n. 8—*Codicis Iuris Canonici Fontes,* cura Emi Petri Card. Gasparri editi (9 vols. [Vols. VII-IX ed. cura et studio Emi Iustiniani Card. Serédi], Romae [postea Civitate Vaticana]: Typis Polyglottis Vaticanis, 1923-1939), n. 682 (hereafter cited *Fontes*).

[18] Can. 253, § 1.

group of Sacramentals. These latter are defined as "sacred objects and actions which the Church, in a certain imitation of the sacraments, employs for the purpose of obtaining especially spiritual favors through its intercession." [19]

Article 2. Church

As has been previously intimated, for a proper understanding of the scope of canon 1181 much depends upon the interpretation given to the word "church." If entrance to the church for sacred rites must be entirely free, as the law states, then it seems that the principal emphasis is being placed by the lawgiver upon a gratuitous attendance at the rites themselves; and that *wherever* these sacred rites are held—commonly in church—there shall be no charge of any kind for admission. To give some endorsement to this opinion, a brief discussion of the word "church" is readily appropriate.

It is immediately evident that a distinction must first be drawn between the technical, canonical sense of the term "church" and the broader concept of the word as envisioned by the masses and sanctioned by common parlance. In its restricted sense, a church is "a sacred edifice dedicated to divine worship, especially with a view to enabling all the faithful to practice therein public worship." [20]

This technical definition, although extremely concise, contains three essential elements, which distinguish churches properly so-called from all other places of worship: namely, a church is a *sacred edifice*, it is open to *all* the faithful, and it is especially destined for the *public* practice of sacred devotions. Divine worship in other places is limited in various degrees by ecclesiastical law.

In a broader sense, then, the term "church" also embraces all other places *specifically set apart* by general law for the performance of divine worship. Such places are known as "oratories." An oratory is defined as "a place destined for divine worship, but not with the principal object of serving the faithful at large for public worship." [21]

[19] Can. 1144.

[20] Can. 1161.

[21] Can. 1188, § 1.

This definition is broad enough to include all three types of oratories (public, semi-public, and private). It is also sufficiently specific to differentiate such oratories (by stating that they are places *destined for divine worship*) from all other places whether sacred or profane.

An oratory is *public* if, though it be erected primarily for the convenience of a certain group of persons, or even for private individuals, rather than for the faithful at large, nevertheless, all the faithful have a right to frequent it—at least at the times of divine services—and may fulfill their obligations therein. A *semi-public* oratory is one which is erected for the convenience of some community or group of the faithful, but to which persons who are not included within the community or the group do not have any *strict right* of admittance at any time. *Private* or *domestic* oratories are those which have been erected in private houses for the exclusive benefit or convenience of some family or individual.[22]

In the widest sense—applicable to the work at hand—the "ecclesia" of canon 1181 may be said to comprehend not only churches and oratories which are strictly such, but also all places where, here and now, divine services or sacred rites are being performed. Naturally such a usage could have an almost unlimited application. Places, in this widest sense, which might be considered under the term "church" include stores, auditoriums, theaters, and other buildings used for Mass and the performance of sacred rites in mission territories, sparsely populated areas, and other localities which do not as yet have their own churches or oratories. The term also includes mobile chapels, places aboard ship where divine services are held (when such places are not already designated as oratories), services conducted "sub dio," and in general all places where the portable altar is actually being used.

In the previous treatment of sacred rites[23] it was concluded that these embraced the Mass, the Sacraments, the Divine Office, and the various Sacramentals. Of these, the most important sacred rite is the Holy Sacrifice of the Mass. Everything in the

[22] Can. 1188, § 2, 1°, 2°, 3°.

[23] Cf. *supra*, pp. 14-19.

Church is centered around the cult of the Eucharist, and when considered from the aspect of "sacrifice" it constitutes, undoubtedly, the principal and fundamental sacred rite of the Church. For this reason the term sacred rites refers principally to the Mass and secondarily to the other devotions. This explains why one thinks primarily of attendance at Mass when one contemplates the term "sacred rites." And, indeed, more has been said and written about the place for Mass than about the places relative to the performance of the other acts of worship. So also one rarely, if ever, hears of a door collection or a charge for attendance at benediction, a baptism, or a wedding, whereas such an abuse is not uncommon in connection with attendance at Mass.

The point of this discussion is the fact that if such abuses occur in places where they are forbidden by the *literal* wording of the canon, one can certainly expect that they may also occur in other places where sacred rites are held. Hence, the purpose at hand is to emphasize the idea that *the lawgiver intends that there shall be no charge for attendance at sacred functions.* The prohibition against any charge for admission therefore extends to all places where these various sacred functions are being held; any restriction here of that prohibition becomes applicable only in so far as certain places are by law excluded from serving any purpose of sacred functions.

Thus, for example, private baptism may be given at any time and in any place.[24] The place, however, for solemn baptism is the baptistry in either a church or a public oratory.[25] The proper place for the administration of the sacrament of confirmation is a church; nevertheless, for a just and reasonable cause the minister may confer the sacrament in any becoming place.[26] Holy Communion may be given in any place where Mass can allowably be said, even in a private oratory, unless the local ordinary should for good reasons have forbidden it in particular cases.[27]

[24] Can. 771.

[25] Can. 773.

[26] Can. 791.

[27] Can. 869.

The proper place for the sacrament of penance is a church or a public or semi-public oratory.[28] The law, however, allows the confessions of women to be received in other places, provided that on the part of these penitents there is some illness or necessity. The freedom which the law itself grants is of course subject to the enacted precautions of the local ordinary. On the other hand, the confessions of men may be heard, provided there is a suitable reason, in almost any place—even in private houses.[29]

In view of the nature of the sacrament of extreme unction, it may be administered in *any* place—even one that would not ordinarily be considered fitting, provided the condition of the subject does not allow him to be moved to a more fitting place.

General ordinations are to be held in the cathedral church. But the bishop may have particular ordinations, for any just reason, in other churches. If possible, they should take place in the principal church of the place; but the bishop may conduct them in the chapel of the seminary, or of the episcopal residence, or of a religious house. First tonsure and minor orders may be conferred even in private oratories.[30]

Marriage between Catholics is to be contracted in the parish church, and is not to take place in another church, public or semi-public oratory without the permission of the ordinary or of the pastor. In an extraordinary case and for a good reason the local ordinary may permit the celebration of such marriages in private houses. Only in case of urgent necessity and with due precaution may he permit marriages to take place in the churches or chapels of seminaries or of women religious. Marriages between Catholics and non-Catholics are to be contracted outside the church (in places left to the discretion of the local ordinary), unless the ordinary sees fit to dispense because he fears that a greater evil would result from enforcing this rule.[31] Specification of the place for the contracting of mixed marriages will thus depend considerably upon local statutes.

[28] Can. 908.

[29] Cf. can. 910, §§ 1, 2.

[30] Can. 1009, §§ 1, 2, 3.

[31] Cf. can. 1109, §§ 1, 2, 3.

Private exposition of the Blessed Sacrament may be held for a good reason, even apart from any special permission of the ordinary, in churches and oratories which have the right to reserve the Blessed Sacrament. Public benediction is allowed in all churches on the Feast of Corpus Christi. At other times it may be given only for a good and serious reason with the permission of the local ordinary, who may also decide where it is to be given.[32]

Thus it can be seen that the place for the administration of the sacraments and sacramentals is defined within certain limits by the law itself. To be remembered, however, is the fact that wherever the sacred rites may allowably be performed there also is the prohibition against any charge for admission to such functions.

Article 3. Free Admission

The phrase "free admission" seems to be so self-explanatory that it needs no further comment. In view, however, of the many abuses which, despite repeated condemnations, persist in a denial of this required freedom of entry, a few remarks are undoubtedly apropos.

To be admitted "free" implies, first of all, that one be allowed to be present for the function in question without having to make a payment of any kind. By way of anticipation, it may be noted here that, after it was first forbidden to take up a collection at the church door, some pastors, seeking to avoid the prohibition, altered their procedure in such a manner that the money was thereafter collected *not at the church door itself,* but from within the vestibule. The Fathers of the II Plenary Council of Baltimore (1866) were aware of this tactic, and they demanded that it be stopped.[33]

Other pastors simply retained the practice. They defended their action by arguing that no one was actually prevented from hearing Mass if he could not make the customary offering. In a special warning directed to the United States in the year 1869, the Sacred Congregation for the Propagation of the Faith ex-

[32] Cf. can. 1274, § 1.

[33] Cf. *infra,* pp. 48-50.

pressed its awareness of this subterfuge. It noted specifically that in some churches "the poor among the faithful are by no means turned away from entering if they have no money to contribute, but they are compelled on account of their poverty to stand thus exposed and humiliated before all to their great embarrassment; so much so, that sometimes many stay away from hearing Mass." [34]

The Admonition then continued with a statement expressing a positive repudiation of such practices: "Since this Sacred Congregation first learned these things, it has not ceased to alert the solicitude of certain bishops against the aforesaid abuses. . . ."

It is plainly evident, from the tone of this and other decrees to be treated later, that every aspect of this problem has been given due consideration by the Holy See. What it desires in this regard goes beyond the ordinary implication of the phrase "free admission." Obviously, the lawgiver intends that the faithful should be accorded gratuitous admission to the church. But, more than that, he demands that they must be *freely admitted to the sacred rites therein.* This later requirement implies that there be no obstacle, hindrance, restraint, or impediment whatsoever to hamper or molest them in any manner as they enter the church.

When entrants are accosted at the church door by being requested to contribute a specific offering or fee, they certainly are not being *freely* admitted, even though they subsequently are allowed to pass without a charge in view of their poverty or simply because they refuse to pay.

The Sacred Congregation was quick to note that the very fact that a collection is taken up at the church door creates a *moral* impediment for some of the faithful. Whether or not it causes them to remain away from Mass is beside the point. Their right, as accorded in the law, is being directly and unjustly restricted.

Moreover, since they are to be freely admitted to the sacred rites, the faithful must be allowed to enter the *nave* or *body* of the church proper without being molested for a fee of any kind. To permit them to come in through the outer doors without a

[34] Cf. *infra,* p. 53.

charge and then to demand a payment at the entrance to the aisles is in direct violation of the law. In one church where *turnstiles* were actually erected at the aisle entrances, the pastor defended the practice by arguing that admission to the church was free; there were no collectors "at the door." The poor and those who did not wish to take a seat were allowed (*forced* would be a better word) to stand in the vestibule. This, he felt, was within the limits of the law.

That one may fulfill his obligation of hearing Mass by assisting in the vestibule is not to be denied.[35] Of more important consideration here, however, is the fact that an abuse such as that described above offends not only against canon 1181, but also against the provision of the III Plenary Council of Baltimore (1884), which demands that in every church there must be some rent-free pews reserved for the convenience or accommodation of the poor.[36]

The particular laws of the Plenary Councils of Baltimore which are not contrary to the Code of Canon Law continue in force.[37]

[35] Cf. Guiniven, *The Precept of Hearing Mass,* The Catholic University of America Canon Law Studies, No. 158 (Washington, D. C.: The Catholic University of America Press, 1942), pp. 103-105.

[36] "In unaquaque ecclesia constituatur spatium liberum ubi fideles Sacro adesse et verbum Dei audire possint. In hoc autem spatio eligendo et in eorum usum aptando, nunquam obliviscatur ille, qui ecclesiae praeest, hos homines esse Christi pauperes, et Boni Pastoris exemplo misericorditer cum illis agat, seduloque vitet quidquid eos contemnendi aut pudefaciendi specimen prae se ferre possit. Secus enim (quod Apostolus expresse vetat), exhonorantur pauperes (Jac. II. 2-6), et timeri aliquando potest ne per pastorem ecclesiae ii, pro quorum aeque ac pro divitum animabus rationem est redditurus, a divino cultu et a vita Christiana penitus arceantur."—*Acta et Decreta Concilii Plenarii Baltimorensis Tertii, A.D. MDCCCLXXXIV* (Baltimorae: Typis Joannis Murphy et Sociorum, 1886), Titulus IX, Caput V, Num. 289 (hereafter cited *III Plen. Conc. Balt.*).

[37] Cf. can. 6. Cf. also Abbo-Hannan, *The Sacred Canons* (2 vols., St. Louis: B. Herder Book Co., 1952), I, 9-10; Cicognani, *Canon Law* (2. ed., Westminster, Maryland: The Newman Press, 1949), pp. 498-502; Woywod-Smith, *A Practical Commentary on the Code of Canon Law* (1. printing, revised and enlarged edition of 2 vols. combined in 1, New York City: Joseph F. Wagner, Inc., 1952), n. 6 (hereafter cited *Practical Commentary*); Barrett, *A Comparative Study of the Councils of Baltimore and the Code of Canon Law,* The Catholic University of America Canon Law

Since the Code mentions nothing about the reservation of free pews, this statute must be considered as *praeter Codicem,* and thus still binding.[38] Certainly, then, the law is contravened when the poor are not accommodated with such free pews; and it is obviously frustrated when they are forcibly detained in the vestibule and not allowed to proceed freely into the church proper, where they might enter these pews.

The vestibule is not, in a technical sense, a part of the church proper. This interpretation is sanctioned by the Code, which, when treating of the violation of churches, indicates that those acts whereby a church is violated must take place *"in ipsa ecclesia."* [39] Commentators are practically unanimous in asserting that such acts which are performed in the vestibule do not constitute a violation of the church.[40] The reasoning behind this deduction is undoubtedly the fact that the sacred rites are performed not in the vestibule, but in the church proper.[41] Inasmuch, then, as the Holy See demands free admission *to the sacred*

Studies, No. 83 (Washington, D. C.: The Catholic University of America, 1932), pp. 20-22 (hereafter cited *A Comparative Study*); Cappello, *Summa Iuris Canonici* (3 vols., Vol. I, editio quinta, Romae: Apud Aedes Universitatis Gregorianae, 1951), I, 57; Michiels, *Normae Generales,* I, 137-138; "Leges particulares, speciales et singulares Codici non oppositae non sunt ullo modo abrogatae a Codice."—Coronata, *Institutiones,* I, n. 1, p. 11.

38 Barrett, *A Comparative Study,* p. 200.

39 Can. 1172, § 1.

40 Bouscaren-Ellis, *Canon Law, A Text and Commentary* (Milwaukee: The Bruce Publishing Company, 1949), p. 595; Augustine, *A Commentary on the New Code of Canon Law* (8 vols., Vol. VI, 2. ed., St. Louis: B. Herder Book Co., 1923), VI, 40 (hereafter cited *A Commentary*); Vermeersch-Creusen, *Epitome* (Vol. II, editio septima, Mechliniae: H. Dessain, 1954), II, n. 489; Abbo-Hannan, *The Sacred Canons,* II, 447; Woywod-Smith, *Practical Commentary,* n. 1213; Gulczynski, *The Desecration and Violation of Churches,* The Catholic University of America Canon Law Studies, No. 159 (Washington, D. C.: The Catholic University of America Press, 1942), pp. 87-88.

41 "In ordinary usage the term 'church' refers to the entire building, but its application in canon 1172, § 1, must be interpreted as meaning that part of the building in which divine services are held. . . . The sacristy is not a part of the church when the term 'church' is understood in its proper meaning; neither is the vestibule or portico. . . ."—Gulczynski, *loc. cit.*

rites, the faithful must accordingly be freely admitted *to the body of the church* where these sacred rites and functions take place.

Article 4. Functions Other Than Sacred Rites Held in Church

Upon integrating the findings of the preceding articles one may conclude that the sacred rites of the Church, in the sense of canon 1181, are the Mass, the Divine Office, the Sacraments, and the Sacramentals. Wherever these rites are performed, in a church, oratory, or elsewhere, no collections are to be taken up at the doors. Nor are there to be any baskets, tables, signs, tickets, or ushers to suggest, ask or request that a donation of any kind be made at the door, in the vestibule, at the entrances to the aisles, or in the aisles themselves. Moreover, the faithful must be freely admitted to the body of the church itself where the sacred functions which they wish to attend will take place.

It should be noted, however, that the demand made by canon 1181 for free admission to the church applies only when sacred rites are being conducted or performed therein.

Sacred places are those which are set apart for divine worship or for the burial of the faithful by way of consecration or blessing as prescribed for that purpose by the approved liturgical books.[42] The very fact that a place is destined for divine services by way of a consecration or blessing implies a prohibition against the performance there of acts not in accord with religion. Considering the church as the principal sacred place (actually an *aedes sacra*), the Code specifically forbids therein all purely profane uses,[43] the performance of impious and sordid acts,[44] business transactions and fairs (*negotiationes et nundinae*), even for pious purposes, and in general whatever is not in keeping with the holiness of the place.[45]

Not to be held in churches, therefore, are such things as dances, banquets, dramatic performances, shows, secular meetings, civil

[42] Can. 1154.

[43] Can. 1164, § 2; can. 1165, § 2.

[44] Can. 1172, § 1, 3°.

[45] Can. 1178.

trials, and the like.[46] There is not, however, any requirement in the law that churches may be used *only* for sacred rites. Various functions which by their nature are neither profane, nor merely secular, nor otherwise forbidden, may be allowed to take place in church, provided they have some connection with religion and are in keeping with the holiness of the place.

Thus, concerts of sacred music, literary or theological disputations, and the conferring of academic diplomas and degrees in a church are not fundamentally and inherently (*per se*) forbidden. Likewise, meetings and congresses of Catholic societies, theological discourses, and the like may also be permitted.[47] Vermeersch-Creusen and Abbo-Hannan make mention of the fact that the Blessed Sacrament should be removed from the tabernacle and transferred to a repository elsewhere while these activities are in progress.[48]

Whenever such non-liturgical functions are being held in the church it is not in opposition to the law to request a moderate admission fee from those attending, provided that these functions have no direct connection with any sacred rite.[49]

[46] Cf. Coronata, *Institutiones* (Vol. II, *De Rebus*, editio quarta, Taurini: Marietti, 1951), II, n. 751; Abbo-Hannan, *The Sacred Canons*, II, 438; Augustine, *A Commentary*, VI, 2-3, 10; Vermeersch-Creusen, *Epitome*, II, n. 491; Ziolkowski, *The Consecration and Blessing of Churches*, The Catholic University of America Canon Law Studies, No. 187 (Washington, D. C.: The Catholic University of America Press, 1943), p. 53.

[47] "Disputationes litterariae vel etiam musicales honestae, collatio graduum academicorum per se non prohibentur, praesertim si de rebus religiosis et scientiis sacris agant, ut ipsa praxis romana admittit."—Coronata, *Institutiones*, II, n. 751. Cf. also Vermeersch-Creusen, *Epitome*, II, n. 491; Cappello, *Summa Iuris Canonici* (Vol. II, editio quinta, Romae: Apud Aedes Universitatis Gregorianae, 1951), II, n. 438; Abbo-Hannan, *The Sacred Canons*, II, 450; Beste, *Introductio in Codicem* (editio tertia, Collegeville, Minn.: St. John's Abbey Press, 1946), pp. 579-582.

[48] Vermeersch-Creusen, *loc. cit.*; Abbo-Hannan, *loc. cit.*

[49] "Sensus genuinus legis non prohibet usum exigendi pretium ad valvas ecclesiae ab illis introeuntibus, qui ex alia quacunque intentione, praeter cultum, in ecclesiam ingredi cupiunt, v. g. ad audiendum concertum musicae sacrae, ad invisenda monumenta. . . . "—Beste, *Introductio in Codicem*, pp. 581-582. Cf. also Cappello, *Summa Iuris Canonici*, II, n. 438; Coronata, *Institutiones*, II, n. 754; Vermeersch-Creusen, *Epitome*, II, n. 491; Abbo-Hannan, *The Sacred Canons*, II, 451.

Sometimes, however, particular laws prohibit a payment even on these occasions. The Provincial Council of the Archdiocese of Utrecht, Holland, held in 1934, contained the following statute:

> We strictly forbid that a church or oratory is ever to be opened for political meetings or gatherings or that they be used for exhibitions of any kind whatsoever, either of music or of singing, for which entrance can be gained only by the payment of a price."[50]

Many European churches contain notable works of art which are frequently on the sight-seeing agenda of most of the tourists. In order to help defray expenses, local law or custom allows a small payment to be asked of those who enter such churches to view these art treasures. Such exhibition periods, however, must occur at times other than those set aside for divine services, and they must not be prejudicial to the law which demands that the churches in which the Blessed Sacrament is kept, especially the parochial churches, must be open to the people for at least a few hours each day.[51]

The 1948 Synod of the Diocese of Madrid in Spain contains the following statute:

> With permission of the ordinary it is permitted that for the payment of a small sum entrance may be had to the notable churches to see the works of art, outside the hours which are given to sacred functions and outside the time when the churches or oratories must remain open daily for visits to the Blessed Sacrament.[52]

In many churches during the hours of such art exhibits the

[50] "Districte prohibemus ecclesiam vel oratorium umquam patere conventui vel coetui politico, vel adhiberi pro exhibitionibus cuiuscumque generis vel musicae vel cantus quae soluto pretio tantum adiri possint."—Cf. *Acta et Decreta Conc. Provincialis Ultraiectensis, anno 1934* (Institutum Surdo-mutorum in Gestel S. Michaelis [no date given]), pag. 138.

[51] Can. 1266.

[52] "Con licencia del Ordinario puede permitirse que, mediante una cuota módica, las iglesias notables por su arte sean visitadas fuera de las horas de las funciones sagradas y del tiempo en que estas iglesias u oratorios han de estar diariamente abiertos para la pública visita del Santísimo Sacramento. (S. C. Prop. Fide, 15 agosto 1869)."—*Sínodo Diocesano de Madrid-Alcalá, anno 1948* [no place or date of publication given], Constitutio 375.

Blessed Sacrament is reserved in a side chapel, which is freely accessible to all at any time.

Among the functions which need to be mentioned here is the preaching of the word of God. In view of its important rôle as the principal means whereby the faithful are instructed in the knowledge and love of God, it merits special consideration in the Code of Canon Law.[53]

It is not the purpose of this dissertation to conclude whether or not preaching is a *sacred rite*. Authors, for the most part, are silent in this respect. Those who do comment, argue only by way of analogy, and there seems to be about an equal weight of opinion on the two sides of the problem.

If preaching *is* a sacred rite, then it comes under the scope of canon 1181; if not, then it remains for the local ordinaries to legislate, as they see fit and if the need arises, regarding collections at the church door on the occasion of such functions.

Regardless of the solution to that problem, if the preaching takes place in connection with some other sacred rite, such as Benediction of the Blessed Sacrament, and the two are joined so that those who come to attend one are present for the other also, then by virtue of association all door collections are outlawed at such services.

When the entire function, however, is given over solely to preaching, such as a sermon, a mission, a triduum, or a *Tre Ore* service, such a function does not in and of itself (*per se*) constitute a sacred rite according to the ordinary understanding of the term.

Nevertheless, in the United States there is a particular prohibition against door collections on the occasion of functions wherein the word of God is preached. The II Plenary Council of Baltimore (1866) forbade collecting from the faithful at the doors of the church whenever they entered to be present for the Sacrifice of the Mass *or to hear the word of God.*[54]

The III Plenary Council of Baltimore (1884) reiterated and strengthened this prohibition in two of its statutes.[55] This pre-

[53] Cf. cans. 1327-1351.

[54] Cf. *infra*, p. 51.

[55] Cf. *infra*, pp. 55-56.

cept of the Baltimore Councils is considered to be *praeter Codicem,* and obliges all in this country even today.[56] Also, the Sacred Congregation for the Propagation of the Faith, in an Admonition addressed to the bishops of the United States in 1869, put forth this same principle:

> . . . Moreover, . . . the Sacred Congregation in desiring to abolish and eliminate [the practice of door collections] entirely, does not now cease to exhort Your Excellency in the Lord . . . that you put forth every effort to see to it that when the faithful enter churches in order to be present at the Divine Mysteries or to hear the Word of God, that, likewise, there be no collectors whatsoever placed at the doors of these same churches.[57]

This calls to mind a practice, which has existed in some places, wherein a noted speaker is scheduled to preach the *Tre Ore* Services on Good Friday afternoon, and those attending are charged an entrance fee of twenty-five or fifty cents, usually because of the "prestige" of the preacher.

It seems that such a practice cannot be tolerated, in view of what has previously been said. And, in addition, the *Tre Ore* Devotions, although they may not constitute a sacred rite, are certainly something very sacred. Even in the minds of the people, this devotion is much more profound than the ordinary function of preaching. This makes the danger of scandal, also, much greater. Pastors should be grateful that their people have sufficient faith to turn out for such services; and they should strive to increase the attendance, rather than to discourage it by taking advantage of so solemn an occasion to enrich the parochial treasury.

With the advent of the Restored Order of Holy Week liturgy this abuse will probably cease because the *Tre Ore* devotions themselves are being discontinued in most places.

[56] Cf. *supra,* pp. 25-26.

[57] Cf. *infra,* p. 53.

CHAPTER IV

BACKGROUND AND EARLY HISTORY

Article 1. Church Support

To determine exactly when and where church door collections first came into being is extremely difficult, if not impossible. The practice is known to have existed in some places in Europe for a great many years. Whether or not it had is origin there cannot be concluded with any degree of definitive certainty. Most of the early clergy in the United States came from Europe, and it is possible that some of them may have introduced the custom in this country after having seen it in operation in their native land. It is also equally possible that there is no connection whatsoever between the beginnings of the practice in this country and its origin elsewhere.

Financing the work of religion has always and everywhere been a great problem for the Church. Providing for its many and varied needs has not been, and probably never will be, an easy task. Even when state support or endowments of one kind or another were in evidence, they usually proved inadequate, so that the faithful themselves were then called upon to supplement the needed income. This was usually done by way of an appeal for freewill offerings and by means of collections of all sorts. Frequently, however, the various *innovations* which sprang up served as a means for meeting the monetary demands of the times.

In the fifteenth century, in England, collection boxes were occasionally placed in churches to attract the donations of the people.

> Collections for specific objects are, perhaps, the most common in all parochial accounts. In one, the holy water vat for the asperges and the thurible are said to have been purchased by collections "made by boys of the parish." In another, that of St. Mary-at-Hill, such collections were very constant; money for "candlesilver" was regular, and for such objects as the new "Rood loft," etc., frequent. . . . Sometimes the wardens placed a collection-box in the church to

> receive general offerings towards parochial expenses. This seems to have led at times to difficulties with the parson, and at one time it was prohibited. Bishop Quevil, of Exeter, for example, says that the practice introduced into some parishes of putting a box, either into the church or outside, to gather alms, has led "to contentions between the rector and his parishioners." . . . The bishop consequently orders that all such collection-boxes be removed from the churches or cemeteries of his diocese at once.[1]

The reason for the command to do away with the collection boxes seems to have been the complaint of the pastors that the people were placing most of their alms in the boxes (which alms were controlled and dispensed by the wardens) instead of contributing to the support of the clergy and the work of religion in general. The fact that these collections took place in the vicinity of the church door does not seem to have influenced the prohibition, but it is precisely this fact which leads to the mention of the practice herein.

Elsewhere, a source of income was the money derived from the payment of pew rent. The custom of renting pews began, in all probability, in Germany about the thirteenth century. Before that time only the clergy, the church patron, and the nobility had seats provided for them. Others stood, knelt, or sat on the floor, as they chose, for divine services. Gradually the people began building individual seats to be used by them while attending church functions. Each person had his own idea as to how such a seat should be built, and he placed it wherever he saw fit in the church. The resultant confusion and the dissimilarity of chairs and benches which cropped up anywhere and everywhere forced the authorities to take action. In striving to bring order out of chaos, uniform seats or pews were erected throughout the church at the expense of the parish. These were then rented or sold to the parishioners for a time or for life. Certain other customs grew up regarding the right of one who bought a pew to rent it to another, the right to pass it on to one's heirs, etc. In fact, the entire system became very complex and exacting.[2]

[1] Gasquet, *Parish Life in Medieval England* (New York: Benziger Brothers, 1906), pp. 128-130.

[2] Grünewald, *Die Rechtsverhältnisse an Kirchenstühlen,* Görres-Gesellschaft zur Pflege der Wissenschaft im katholischen Deutschland (Hefte 1-5,

Early in the present century, the Bishop of Paderborn (Germany) initiated legislation to suppress the custom of pew rent. He was opposed by many of the people and principally by those who had previously "bought" their pews for life. Some even sought compensation from the Church, through process of the civil law, for the "rights" which were being taken away from them. The bishop petitioned the Holy See for advice. On December 11, 1920, the Sacred Congregation of the Council issued a reply which upheld the bishop's action and declared that the people, in going to the civil authorities, had acted improperly. The bishop was urged, however, to exercise due care in doing away with the renting of pews in such places where the custom was of long-standing duration.[3]

Not all countries have pews in their churches even today. In some of these places a supply of chairs or seats is available at the rear of the church for those who wish such a convenience during divine services. For their use a small offering is generally asked. These contributions go into the parish fund, or for the upkeep of widows, or toward the help of the poor.

> The practice of renting pews is a German development, and outside of the United States has never become general in any other country, at least in Europe. Even up to the present time, pews have not been introduced as common fixtures in churches in the Latin countries. Consequently there can be no question of renting them. Instead of pews single, portable chairs are generally found, and for their use seat-money may be asked.[4]

In France this custom of seat money seems to be immemorial. On May 18, 1806, Cardinal Cambacérès, Archbishop of Rouen in France (1802-1818), issued a decree (*imperiale decretum*) having to do with assigning places or seats in church. Title I, Article I, of the decree read as follows:

Köln: Verlag und Druck von T. P. Bachem, 1908; Heft 6- , Paderborn: Druck und Verlag von Ferdinand Schöningh, 1909- , Heft 49 (1927), pp. 1-62.

[3] *Acta Apostolicae Sedis, Commentarium Officiale* (Romae, 1909-1929; Civitate Vaticana, 1929-), XIII (1921), 262-268 (hereafter cited *AAS*).

[4] Kremer, *Church Support in the United States*, p. 74.

> All churches are open freely to the public; hence, it is expressly forbidden to receive anything within the churches and at their entrance, other than the price of the chairs, under any pretext whatsoever.[5]

These three methods of support: various collections, pew rents and seat money, have greatly supplemented the ordinarily inadequate income of the Church in many places. Certainly there have been other more important sources of revenue, such as endowments, bequests, assessments, tithes, and the like. But only the former three have a direct connection with the present treatise. Considered in themselves, they are all approved means of financing the work of religion; however, the manner in which they have been operative has not always been above suspicion. Indeed in some places the entire system of "entrance fees" may be traced to the improper employment of one or more of these otherwise legitimate practices.

Article 2. The First References to Door Collections in the United States

The problem of providing for the temporal needs of the Church in its earliest years in the United States was an almost insurmountable one. Catholics were few in number, and for the most part their financial resources were extremely limited. Nationality differences often led to open schism against proper authority, and as a result monetary support was not provided for many parishes from time to time.

Progress was difficult. Although the sacrifices of the faithful came to fruition with the erection of new churches, all to often their efforts were offset by the violent outbursts of anti-Catholic mobs who set fire to church buildings and damaged other ecclesiastical institutions beyond repair.[6]

[5] "Les églises sont ouvertes gratuitement au public; en conséquence, il est expressément défendu de rien percevoir, dans les églises et à leur entrée, de plus que le prix des chaises, sous quelque pretéxte que ce soit."—This information was forwarded to the writer by the present Archbishop of Rouen, the Most Reverend Joseph Marie Martin; no further information was included.

[6] The burning of the Charlestown convent is a typical example of such mob violence. Cf. Lord-Sexton-Harrington, *History of the Archdiocese of*

In an effort to secure necessary funds and to distribute the burden of upkeep equally among all, some pastors instituted the practice of taking up a collection at the church doors. This had the effect of obtaining at least some contribution from many who otherwise would have given nothing toward church support in the regular collection.

Shortly after the turn of the present century, an article appearing in *The Ecclesiastical Review* made the following observation in commenting on the problem:

> The custom of collecting a specified fee at the church door from those who are not regular seat-holders, or who cannot be relied upon to comply in other ways with the demands to supply the parochial needs, has grown of late years. It is tolerated in spite of the prohibition of our Plenary Councils, and is sought to be justified on the ground that the people understand and approve the system as the easiest way of enforcing reasonable compliance with the divine law which obliges one to support religion in proportion to his ability and the needs of his parish.[7]

The very first reference to a practice of this sort, and which the author was able to discover, was made on the occasion of the I Synod of the Diocese of Boston, held in 1842. The eighteenth statute of that synod prohibited collecting money or tickets (previously purchased) from the faithful at the doors of churches whenever they entered to hear Mass or attend other sacred functions.[8]

Boston in the Various Stages of Its Development, 1604 to 1943 (3 vols., New York: Sheed & Ward, 1944), II, 205-239 (hereafter cited *History of Boston*). Cf. also Shea, *History of the Catholic Church in the United States* (4 vols., New York, 1886-1892), II, 462-494.

[7] Anonymous, "Collecting Money at Church Doors Unconditionally Abolished," *The Ecclesiastical Review* (*American Ecclesiastical Review*, Vols. I-XXXII, Philadelphia, 1889-1905; *The Ecclesiastical Review*, Vols. XXXIII-CIX, Philadelphia, 1905-1943; *The American Ecclesiastical Review*, Vol. CX- , Washington, D. C., 1944-), XLV (1911), 592 (hereafter cited *The American Ecclesiastical Review* and *The Ecclesiastical Review respectively*).

[8] *Synodus Dioecesana, Bostoniensis I, 21 aug. 1842* (Bostoniae: Ex Typis Patritii Donahoe [no publication date given]), Num. XVIII. For the text of this statute, cf. *infra*, p. 63.

Attempts to obtain more information about the practice proved unsuccessful. None of the histories which the author perused shed any light on the subject beyond listing door collections among the things forbidden by the Synod of 1842. This leads to the conclusion that the practice was in no way widespread at the time. And from the nature and growth of the Catholicity in the Boston area in the 1840's, the Church there appears to have been on a relatively sound footing, economically.[9]

Although the Diocese of Boston had seen many lean years earlier, by the time of the I Synod the financial outlook had improved considerably, in consequence of the excellent administration of the second bishop of that See, the Most Reverend Benedict Joseph Fenwick (1782-1846).

> Benedict Joseph Fenwick may be called the organizer of the Diocese of Boston. Under him there first came to be priests, laity, churches, and resources enough to constitute a viable and a fairly strong diocese. . . . He was a particularly good financial manager, adverse to all extravagance, holding himself and his priests to "get along with what they had," regarding a debt as a nightmare and yet not unwilling to risk one when there seemed a reasonable chance of paying it off quickly and the object was of great importance. During his early years here his income was extremely meagre, coming almost entirely from the revenues of the Cathedral and from his own inherited property in Maryland. From the early thirties onward, however, thanks to the immense growth of the Cathedral congregation, he found himself in possession of much more ample means. Although these were always too circumscribed to suit his purposes, still, they freed him from the severe worries he had had in the beginning and allowed him to carry through such large enterprises as the Benedicta settlement or the

[9] ". . . the situation of the diocese at the end of the Fenwick era in 1846 presented a most heartening contrast to that of the beginning in 1825. Instead of the initial nine churches, there were forty-eight in use or virtually completed. Instead of three priests, there were thirty-nine. The number of the faithful was estimated at seventy thousand. Among the twenty-five dioceses of the United States, Boston stood eleventh in the number of dedicated churches and seventh in the number of priests, and it was tied with Detroit for fifth place as regards total Catholic population." —Lord-Sexton-Harrington, *History of Boston,* II, 294.

founding of Holy Cross College. It was no financially encumbered heritage that he left to his successor.[10]

This argues favorably for the generosity of the faithful in the diocese, and tends to discount their indifference or lack of cooperation—reasons given for beginning door collections elsewhere. In all probability, it had been brought to the bishop's attention that one or two churches had begun such a system; and in the I Synod he forbade the practice in order to keep it from being instituted elsewhere.

In 1855, the Reverend F. X. Weninger, S.J., published a book of directions concerning pastoral duties and administration, drawn from the decrees of the Baltimore Councils, which had been approved by the Holy See, and from the provisions of various diocesan synods held in this country up to that time. This he said was done at the request of many priests who long desired such a work. Contained among the rules was the following reference to door collections:

> Collectae tum ordinariae tum extraordinariae pro Ecclesia fiant ab Aedituis assistentibus intra Missam ad Offertorium, nisi in casu extraordinario aliter visum fuerit.
>
> Absolute autem non convenit, ut collectae fiant foris ad januam, neque pro casu extraordinario, multo minus ut non solventes unquam ab ingressu in Ecclesiam prohibeantur.[11]

This provision was probably drawn solely from the I Synod of the Diocese of Boston, because none of the previous Councils of Baltimore had legislated concerning door collections, nor, in so far as can be determined, was the practice mentioned in any of the other diocesan synods which had been held up to that time.

Subsequently, what seems to have been the very next reference to the practice of collecting money at the doors of churches is contained in a letter written February 19, 1859, by His Eminence Alexander Cardinal Barnabo, Prefect of the Sacred Congregation for the Propagation of the Faith. Although the letter itself —most probably addressed to the Most Reverend John Baptist

[10] *Ibid.*, pp. 295-296.

[11] Weninger, *Epitome Pastoralis ad Usum Cleri in Statibus Foederatis Americae* (Buffalone: Typis C. Wieckmann & S. Brandt, 1855), Pars I, Titulus Tertius, Caput I, Num. XXI.

Purcell, Archbishop of Cincinnati—cannot be located, it is cited in the *Acta,* or Official Acts, of the III Provincial Council of Cincinnati (April 29–May 5, 1861).[12]

The nature of the letter seems to have been a request that the Archbishop diligently investigate the reported practice that in some areas of his archdiocese the faithful were being charged at the door of the church for admittance to divine worship.

On April 30, 1861, at the Second Public Assembly of the aforementioned Council, it was the first of several topics proposed for discussion. From the Acts of the Council it is apparent that the practice in question existed in three lakeshore towns (*"oppidis maritimis"*) of the Diocese of Cleveland, and that the Bishop of Cleveland himself was heard concerning the matter.[13]

The following day, at the Third Private Assembly, the Fathers of the Council passed judgment upon the situation, having heard the opinions of the various theologians who had considered it. They concluded that the practice, as it existed in the Cleveland Diocese, proposed no great difficulties, since no one was actually prevented from entering the church. Nor, it was held, was anyone impeded from the reception of the sacraments or from hearing the word of God. It was therefore suggested that the Bishop of Cleveland, after consulting the clergy and people of the three towns in question, should use his prudent judgment to decide whether the innovation should be retained or relinquished. It should be noted, however, that although the practice was not condemned by the Council, neither was it given positive approbation. In fact, it was very strongly urged that it not be expanded.[14] There is no further mention of the situation, nor does it appear in any of the twelve Decrees of the Council.

12 *Acta et Decreta Quatuor Conciliorum Provincialium Cincinnatensium 1855-1882* (Cincinnati: Typis Benziger Fratrum, 1886), p. 113 (hereafter cited *Acta Conc. Prov. Cincin.*); *Acta et Decreta Sacrorum Conciliorum Recentiorum, Collectio Lacensis* (7 vols., Friburgi Brisgoviae, 1870-1892), III, 220d (hereafter cited *Coll. Lac.*).

13 ". . . auditisque variis theologorum sententiis, atque imprimis audito, Rm̃o Episcopo Clevelandensi, in cujus dioecesi hujusmodi praxis existet [!], sed in tribus tantum oppidis maritimis . . ."—*Acta Conc. Prov. Cincin., loc. cit.; Coll. Lac., loc. cit.*

14 "RRm̃i Patres Concilii . . . relinquunt *prudenti sapientiae,* Rm̃i Episcopi Clevelandensis, . . . judicantes tamen nullatenus expedire, ut [praxis

On January 2, 1862, the Sacred Congregation for the Propagation of the Faith issued a Decree to the effect that the Acts and Decrees of the III Provincial Council of Cincinnati would be approved, subject to the incorporation of certain changes and corrections, which were, in fact, forwarded nineteen days later. There is no reference to "door collections" in either the official Decree or the letter containing this list of changes.

Shortly after the above noted communications, there follows the most important document that appeared up to then. Indeed, it is the first significant step on the part of the Holy See toward positive legislation demanding for all a gratuitous access to church. Cardinal Barnabo penned this communique, dated January 27, 1862, to the Archbishop of Cincinnati. In it he stated that the Holy Father (Pope Pius IX) was displeased after reading about the practice of demanding money at the church door, and he (the Pope) decreed that it should be stopped within two years. The words of the letter are themselves so significant that it seems fully warranted to quote, in part, what Cardinal Barnabo then wrote:

> Post ea quae circa Synodi Acta per literas diei 21. labentis Mensis Tibi significavi, addendum superest SSño. Dño. Papae relata fuisse inter caetera quae in tertia Congne. privata Synodi leguntur circa praxim exigendi pecuniam ad fores Ecclesiarum in tribus Oppidis Maritimis Dioecesis Clevelandensis. Porro etsi Sanctitas Sua Synodi Cincinnatensis decreta, juxta modum a S. Congregatione jam expressum, confirmaverit, in eo tamen quod memoratam praxim attingit, declaravit hanc Sibi minime placere, ideoque per literas S. Congregationis moneri voluit Episcopum Clevelandensem, ut intra spatium duorum annorum dictam praxim a sua Dioecesi eliminare studeat, aliaque ratione provideat sustentationi parochorum. . . .[15]

---

invecta] ad alias ecclesias, in quibus nondum viget, extendatur."—*Acta Conc. Prov. Cincin.*, pp. 113-114; *Coll. Lac.*, III, 220d-221a.

[15] *Acta Conc. Prov. Cincin.*, p. 133; *Coll. Lac.*, III, 229a-230a; *Juris Pontificii de Propaganda Fide Pars Secunda Complectens Decreta Instructiones Encyclicas Literas Etc. ab Eadem Congregatione Lata* (cura ac studio Raphaelis De Martinis, 1 vol., Romae, 1909), MXXV, p. 631 (hereafter cited *II Juris Pontificii*).

Historians give a brief account of the happenings in the Cleveland Diocese in this regard, and they advance the reasoning behind the inauguration of these door collections during the incumbency of the Most Reverend Louis Amadeus Rappe (1801-1877), first Bishop of Cleveland (1847-1870).

> Another problem about which Bishop Rappe was concerned had to do with the method of supporting the churches in the larger towns, where the population was not as stable as in the country districts.
>
> For the usual custom of quarterly pew rent the Bishop had substituted the practice of collecting a small seat fee at the entrance to the church on Sundays before the High Mass. Provision was made that no one would be excluded who could not pay the fee. It was hoped that, with the constant coming and going of transients, everyone in this way would have the opportunity of contributing his proper share for the support of the church buildings. The system was not liked by some, who denounced it. The council listened to the Bishop's explanation of the situation and seemed inclined to allow it in the circumstances but would restrict the practice to the "maritime cities" of Cleveland, Sandusky, and Toledo. The Congregation of the Propaganda in Rome, however, forbade it, and it was only after Bishop Rappe explained the case to the Holy Father himself that it was permitted for a time on account of the great financial needs.[16]

The Church in Cleveland certainly had its financial problems, just as the Church did everywhere in those early formative years. When Bishop Rappe took possession of his newly-erected diocese in 1847, he found but one frame church and one priest in the See city.[17]

On Sunday, October 29, 1848, the cornerstone was laid for a new cathedral.[18] Another historian's account of the door collecting incident points out the fact that the difficulties experi-

[16] Hynes, *History of the Diocese of Cleveland, Origin and Growth (1847-1952)* (Diocese of Cleveland: World Publishing Company, 1953), p. 102 (hereafter cited *History of the Diocese of Cleveland*).

[17] Houck, *A History of Catholicity in Northern Ohio and in the Diocese of Cleveland from 1749 to December 31, 1900* (2 vols. [Vol. II: Michael Carr, *Biographical*], Cleveland: Press of J. B. Savage, 1903), I, 78-79.

[18] *Ibid.*, p. 80.

enced by the bishop in financing the cathedral project led to his instituting the practice in question.

> Bishop Rappe found it difficult to meet the expenses of his first Cathedral congregation, in old St. Mary's church, and later in St. John's Cathedral, as many of the parishioners did not contribute their fair share towards the support of the church. He therefore directed that the sum of ten cents be collected from every adult, at the church door, before Mass on Sundays and Holydays of Obligation. To this also the Germans strenuously objected. Finally Father Weninger . . . brought the matter to the attention of the authorities at Rome, who then directed the Bishop to abolish that regulation, so offensive to the Germans, and, in fact, to all.[19]

Bishop Rappe, although of French birth, was intensely American in spirit. He sought to make English the common language of his diocese. In this attempt he antagonized the German immigrants; and relations were not helped when the bishop refused to allow them to erect a separate church at Fremont, where their native tongue could be spoken.[20] This probably explains why he was opposed by the Germans in the door collection project.

Moreover, the bishop abolished the pew rent custom, and in its place he substituted a seat money collection at the church door. It has been previously pointed out that the renting of pews was of a German origin. This innovation, therefore, undoubtedly "added insult to injury."

The bishop's reasoning was logical. Pews were rented for use by the lessee at the parochial or principal Mass only. Thus, if a parish contained fifteen hundred adult souls and the church seated five hundred, there could be, at most, five hundred rentals. The remaining one thousand parishioners obtained rent-free pews at the other scheduled Masses. But by means of a seat money collection, everyone in effect paid a weekly rent at whatever Mass he attended. Fundamentally (*per se*) this was not a violation of any law in force at the time. The collection, however, was taken up *at the church door,* which made the whole system odious.

[19] *Ibid.*, p. 90.

[20] *Ibid.*, pp. 89-90.

From the first account reported above, it is learned that the practice was limited to the cities of Cleveland, Toledo, and Sandusky (the three "lakeshore towns" referred to in the Acts of the III Provincial Council of Cincinnati; all three cities are located on Lake Erie.)

At the time the complaint was made to the Holy See there were only two churches and one small chapel in Toledo,[21] and only two churches in Sandusky.[22] In the city of Cleveland itself there were no more than five churches, the second of which (St. John's Cathedral) was consecrated as late as November 7, 1852.[23] From this it can be deduced that the practice of collecting at the door was extremely limited in extent, and the III Provincial Council of Cincinnati strongly urged that it not be expanded.

After pondering the prohibition which emanated from the Holy See, on weighing in particular the wording of Cardinal Barnabo's letter, and upon considering the background and other developments previously mentioned, one obviously may conclude that the incident in question may well mark the very first time the Holy See became aware of the existence of such a practice anywhere in the universal Church. Certainly the silence of the jurists and commentators in this matter through the previous centuries argues in behalf of this opinion. And although the I Synod of the Diocese of Boston made mention of door collections, its decrees probably were never seen by the Holy See. It was the law then, as now, that only the Acts and Decrees of Provincial and Plenary Councils needed to be sent to Rome for revision and recognition.[24]

Under the second bishop of Cleveland (1872-1891), the Most Reverend Richard Gilmour (1824-1891), the VI Diocesan Synod was held (May 23-25, 1882).

> It was the most important one in the history of the diocese. Present were 139 priests. . . . The ordinances of the Councils of Cincinnati and of Baltimore were recognized, and Bishop Gilmour by his own decree gave force of di-

[21] *Ibid.*, pp. 638-665.

[22] *Ibid.*, pp. 603-614.

[23] *Ibid.*, pp. 195-295.

[24] Cf. can. 291, § 1.

ocesan law to 262 statutes. One hundred of these were printed in pamphlet form as the *Rules and Directions for the Administration of the Temporal and Spiritual Affairs.*[25]

Among the directives contained in this pamphlet is the following one relative to church door collections:

> Door collections are not allowed in any church in this Diocese. Where pews are not rented, and the income is raised by voluntary contributions, collections shall be taken in the pews only, but never at the door or by collectors standing at the foot of the aisles.[26]

In defense of the men who *first* began these practices, it must be stated that they acted, in all probability, in good faith. They saw the great financial needs of their day, and they sought by every means possible to cope with the tasks assigned to them. Perhaps to their way of thinking there was little difference between taking up seat money in the body of the church and taking it up at the church door. Many, even today, still share this same opinion. However, in the early part of the nineteenth century the laws which today regulate matters of this sort had not yet been formulated.

Certainly, then, those ecclesiastical pioneers should not be condemned *ex post facto* for the innovations to which they resorted, often in sheer desperation, and most probably with a clear conscience. And indeed they should not be viewed in the same light as the modern day money changers in the temple who have perpetrated upon their people practices and methods far more reprehensible than those of a century ago, despite the many prohibitions which have come forth between then and now to indicate clearly and beyond all doubt the absolute desire of the Holy See to prevent or abolish any and every abuse of this sort.

[25] Hynes, *History of the Diocese of Cleveland,* p. 158.

[26] *Rules and Directions for the Administration of the Temporal and Spiritual Affairs of Churches, Schools, etc., in the Diocese of Cleveland* (Cleveland: M. R. M'Cabe, 1882), No. 205.

CHAPTER V

LEGISLATION OF THE SECOND PLENARY COUNCIL OF BALTIMORE

ARTICLE 1. BACKGROUND AND IMPORTANCE OF THE COUNCIL

The mainstay of ecclesiastical legislation is, of course, the universal law of the Church. This, however, is supplemented in various ways by the norms and statutes enacted in plenary and provincial councils. Often these latter are of an immediately more important nature than the former, inasmuch as they indicate, as it were, the status of ecclesiastical discipline on the local level. They also demonstrate how universal legislation is reconciled with local custom, and they provide an insight into the various problems of the locality from the manner in which they implement or mitigate the universal law in particular situations.

The Code of Canon Law itself defines the business of these lesser councils. It declares that the Fathers of a plenary or of a provincial council shall diligently investigate the needs and provide appropriate measures in regard to the fostering of the faith, the safeguarding of good morals, the correcting of abuses, the settling of controversies, the maintaining or introducing of uniform observances, and whatever else may appear opportune in reference to the exigencies of their respective territories.[1]

After the displeasure of the Holy Father had been evoked by the practice of exacting money at the church door, the next official convocation to be held in the United States was the II Plenary Council of Baltimore, convoked and presided over by the seventh bishop of that Episcopal See (1864-1872), the Most Reverend Martin John Spalding (1810-1872). The Feast of the Most Holy Rosary, Sunday, October 7, 1866, marked the opening date of its First Solemn Session.

In preparation for this great event, the Archbishop had obtained copies of recent European conciliar legislation. In 1865 he wrote:

[1] Can. 290.

> I have procured copies of some dozen provincial and diocesan councils, held in Europe from 1850 to 1860, and I must confess that, in comparison with them, ours appear very meagre, especially in moral and doctrinal exposition, which in them occupies much space. We have very much to do to lay deeply and solidly the foundations of our canon law. Until now we seem not to have advanced far beyond the rudiments.[2]

Speaking of this forthcoming Council in another letter, Archbishop Spalding pointed out its great importance and summarized what he envisioned as its far-reaching outcome:

> I have thought of embodying in the Council a succinct exposition of doctrine, together with the condemnation of current heresies and errors, as well as suitable rules for the regulation of moral conduct and discipline. . . . I have thought, also, of making our approaching Council a complete repertory of our canon law, embracing, in systematic order, all our previous enactments in the Baltimore councils, together with such canons of provincial and diocesan synods as we may wish to make of general application. In a word, of making it a sort of *corpus juris* for the American Church; throwing into an appendix all Roman rescripts and decisions which have reference to our affairs.[3]

These letters demonstrate the minute detail which accompanied the preparation for this great council. Its decrees may be expected to embody a comprehensive picture of the nation's problems and correspondingly appropriate legislative measures.

The importance of this Plenary Council has been noted in order that its enactments may be appreciated in their true light. Prior to acceptance, they were subjected, in the various Public and Private Sessions, to extensive discussion on the part of the prelates and theologians who were assembled from the entire country.[4] Apart from giving one an insight into the reasons be-

[2] J. L. Spalding, *The Life of the Most Rev. M. J. Spalding, D.D., Archbishop of Baltimore* (New York [no publication date given]), p. 302.

[3] *Ibid.*, p. 301.

[4] "On the 7th of October, 1866, seven archbishops, thirty-eight bishops, three mitred abbots, and over one hundred and twenty theologians met in Baltimore to take part in the deliberations of the Second Plenary Council of the Church in the United States. This was, at the time, the largest

hind the particular laws and the extent of the various abuses, the decrees of this Council comprise, in effect, a considerable part of the law of the Church for the United States.[5]

The Reverend S. B. Smith (1845-1895), a former Professor of Canon Law at Seton Hall Seminary, summarized very succinctly the thoughts put forth above when he wrote:

> To induct into this country Canon Law in its old form, may not be altogether practicable.
>
> Ours is a land in which the Church is placed in peculiar circumstances. Religion is only building up as yet. There are no long-established usages to go by, and no well-defined precedents to follow; while in most parts of Europe, Catholic faith has ruled supreme for generations.
>
> While therefore striving to adhere as closely as possible to the spirit of the Common Law of the Church, we may be obliged at times to deviate from it as to the letter.
>
> This adaptation of Canon Law to our country, it seems to us, has been admirably brought about by the late [Second] Plenary Council of Baltimore.[6]

Article 2. Development of the Decree Demanding Gratuitous Access

After sending out letters of convocation, Archbishop Spalding asked the prelates to submit a list of topics which they deemed prudent to present for the consideration of the committee appointed to prepare the *agenda* for the council. The Sacred Congregation for the Propagation of the Faith, on January 31, 1866,

---

conciliary assembly since the Council of Trent, with the exception of two or three meetings of the bishops in Rome, which, however, were not councils in any proper sense of the word."—*Ibid.*, p. 304.

[5] "These *Acta et Decreta* [of the Baltimore Councils] have all been published (in Latin); they form the basis for a history of canonical legislation and contain the guiding principles of an adequate interpretation of the progress of ecclesiastical discipline in the United States since the creation of the American hierarchy."—Guilday, *A History of the Councils of Baltimore (1791-1884)* (New York, 1932), p. 9. "These, then [the published Acts and Decrees of the Baltimore Councils], are the official texts for the study of our national conciliar legislation, and they form the *Corpus Juris* of the ecclesiastical law of the land."—*Ibid.*, p. 12.

[6] S. B. Smith, *Notes on the Second Plenary Council of Baltimore* (New York, 1874), pp. v-vi.

issued an Instruction containing a list of topics which it, also, proposed for deliberation.

The matter of "door collections" was not suggested by the Sacred Congregation, but it appeared as No. 426 on the preliminary *agenda* of the decrees. At the Tenth Private Assembly, the Fathers of the Council amended the wording of this tentative decree before presenting it, along with the other Acts and Decrees, for the approval of the Holy See.

Although the original wording is not available,[7] several things can be learned from the Notary's record of the proceedings of this private session. First, it appears that the practice of collecting money at the church door was becoming more widespread. It also seems probable that it was discovered, in some form or other, in the Archdioceses of Cincinnati and New York as well as in the Diocese of Cleveland. Secondly, after a study of the overall picture, it can be conjectured that the text, as first drawn up, read—in effect—as follows:

> We [the Fathers of the Council] declare that the practice of demanding money from the faithful at the doors of churches, even if no one (*etiam si nullus*) is impeded from entering therein and being present for divine services, is to be abolished.

At this private session the bishops discussed the problem in detail. It is stated that Cincinnati, Cleveland, and New York brought to light and developed various pertinent considerations. After hearing them, the Fathers of the Council voted to change the wording of the decree in order to make it more forceful, and at the same time more comprehensive. The final draft, as sent to Rome, may be assumed to have read thus:

> We [the Fathers of the Council] declare that the practice, *wherever and in whatever way it exists* (*si qua existat*), of demanding money at the doors of churches, *in such a manner that anyone* (*ita ut ullus*) is impeded from entering therein and being present for divine services, is to be abolished.[8]

[7] Only the final, corrected version of the Decrees, as approved by the Sacred Congregation for the Propagation of the Faith, has been published.

[8] "Ad Num. 426, cum Cincinnatensis, Clevelandensis, et Neo-Eboracensis quaedam explicassent, verba 'siqua existat' post 'praxim' linea 1 addita

This choice in the change of wording appears to have been a very excellent one. In itself it seems to indicate some of the problems considered in this connection by the aforementioned bishops.

The situation, as it existed in the Diocese of Cleveland, has been treated previously.[9] The conclusion reached by the Fathers of the Council of Cincinnati was that the practice of taking money at the door of the church, in the manner in which it was done in the Diocese of Cleveland, caused no problem, since no one was actually prevented from entering the church or impeded from the reception of the sacraments or from hearing the word of God. Nevertheless, Pope Pius IX frowned upon the practice and ordered that it be abolished.

It was probably brought out by the bishops at the Council of Baltimore that in some churches money was asked for not at the door itself, but from just inside the door, or that in other places money was not literally "asked for" at all, but that ushers "silently" extended a collection basket to each parishioner as he arrived, thereby escaping—in each case—the letter of the prohibition in the strictest sense.

These considerations, together with others, undoubtedly led to the insertion of the words *si qua existat* in the decree.

As stated above, the earlier conclusion in relation to Cleveland was ordered abolished despite the fact that it contained a clause conveying the idea that "no one was impeded from entering church." This concept was therefore worked into the rough draft of the Baltimore decree, to the effect that the practice was to be eliminated "*even though* no one was impeded from entering the church."

In order to make the law even more inclusive, and undoubtedly

---

sunt, et 'etiamsi nullus' 2 linea in 'ita ut ullus' mutata. Decretum sic emendatum Patribus placuit."—from the Notary's record of the proceedings of the Tenth Private Assembly—*Concilii Plenarii Baltimorensis II., in Ecclesia Metropolitana Baltimorensi, a die VII. ad diem XXI. Octobris, A. D., MDCCCLXVI., Habiti, et a Sede Apostolica Recogniti, Acta et Decreta* (Baltimorae, 1868), p. lxxxi (hereafter cited *II Plen. Conc. Balt.*); see also *Coll. Lac.*, III, 363c.

[9] *Supra*, pp. 38-44.

being moved by the plight of the poor, lest their embarrassment keep them from attending Mass as a result of the practice of "door collections," the Fathers of the Council changed the phrase *etiamsi nullus* to *ita ut ullus.* They thereby made evident their consideration of the fact that one may be *morally* impeded as well as by physical means.

On October 21, 1866, together with a letter of greeting and explanation, the Acts and Decrees of the Council were submitted for the approval of His Holiness, Pope Pius IX.[10]

Article 3. Revision and Final Form

The Holy Father acknowledged the receipt of the Acts and Decrees in a letter dated September 2, 1867.[11] He, in turn, transmitted them to the Sacred Congregation for the Propagation of the Faith for a due consideration.

On January 24, 1868, Cardinal Barnabo formulated a Decree of Recognition for the Council, in which he stated that, after diligent investigation, the Sacred Congregation saw fit to approve the Acts and Decrees, subject to a few corrections and observations.[12]

Number 18 in the list of revisions, contained in another letter of January 24, 1868, referred to the matter of "door collections" as treated in Decree Number 426 of the Baltimore Council.

It may be recalled that this decree, as submitted to the Holy See, stated—in effect—that *the Fathers of the Council* declared that the practice in question was to be done away with.[13]

The Sacred Congregation noted that it had carefully considered the proceedings of the Council in this matter, as well as all that had transpired theretofore. It particularly stressed the fact that *the Holy Father* had previously declared that the practice of demanding money at the door of the church, in order that the faithful might enter therein, was in no way pleasing to him. Therefore the Sacred Congregation commanded that all bishops should strive diligently to abolish any custom or practice of this

[10] *II Plen. Conc. Balt.*, pp. cxxvii-cxxxii; *Coll. Lac.*, III, 374d-378a.

[11] *II Plen. Conc. Balt.*, pp. cxxxiii-cxxxv; *Coll. Lac.*, III, 377b-379a.

[12] *II Plen. Conc. Balt.*, p. cxxxvi; *Coll. Lac.*, III, 379a.

[13] Cf. *supra*, p. 48.

sort. And to this end it was demanded that the wording of the Baltimore Decree be amended in order that due emphasis might be given to the idea that it was *the Holy Father himself* who declared that this abuse must be eliminated.[14]

The Fathers of the Council of Baltimore made the necessary corrections, and then formulated the official decree. In so doing, they called to mind—by virtue of a footnote included in the official text itself—the letter written some six years earlier by Cardinal Barnabo to the Archbishop of Cincinnati, expressing for the first time the displeasure evidenced by the Supreme Pontiff over the policy of "door collections." [15]

Also included in the text is a statement to the effect that experience has shown wherein other methods can be found to support the Church. This seems to indicate that the Fathers of the Council were confronted with arguments based, in various ways, upon "the need for revenue." By including the foregoing concept in the decree itself, they thwarted, by anticipation, any future pleas on the part of those who might be striving—by means of this defense—for the retention of the practice.

In the measure in which the Sacred Congregation had made various consolidations and eliminations in the preceding statutes, the prohibition of "door collections" was ultimately promulgated as the 397th Decree of the Second Plenary Council of Baltimore. It reads as follows:

> Praxim, si qua existat, pecuniam exigendi ad fores ecclesiarum, ut fideles ingredi possint, et divinis mysteriis adesse, "Sibi minime placere declaravit Summus Pontifex, Pius Papa Nonus, et eliminandam prorsus voluit." Supremi itaque Pastoris judicio obsequentes, huic consuetudini finem imponi omnino volumus. Cum enim alia ratione reditus satis amplos ecclesias percipere posse experientia constet, praxis ea improbanda videtur, quae pecuniae fixam summam, vectigalis instar, fidelibus imponendi, ut Missae adstare vel Verbum Dei audire possint, speciem praeseferre videtur.[16]

[14] *II Plen. Conc. Balt.*, p. cxli, n. 18; *Coll. Lac.*, III, 381c, n. 18.

[15] Cf. *supra*, p. 40. Since this letter has been treated previously, reference to it in the place cited in the official decree will be omitted.

[16] *II Plen. Conc. Balt.*, Titulus VII, Caput II, Num. 397, p. 205; *Coll. Lac.*, III, 506c-d.

CHAPTER VI

THE SPECIAL ADMONITION FROM THE SACRED CONGREGATION FOR THE PROPAGATION OF THE FAITH

On August 15, 1869, little more than a year and a half after the Acts and Decrees of the Second Plenary Council of Baltimore were corrected, approved, and dispatched from Rome, the Sacred Congregation for the Propagation of the Faith was forced to issue still another warning, in the form of an official Admonition (*"Monitum"*), to the United States regarding the matter of collecting money at the church door.[1]

The Decree is extremely terse, yet sacrifices nothing by way of comprehensiveness. And, being couched in no mean terms, it purports to be the most cogent and absolute condemnation of the practice thus far.

It cites the previous declarations on the part of the Holy Father and the same Sacred Congregation, in connection with the approval of the Acts and Decrees of the Third Provincial Council of Cincinnati [2] and of the Second Plenary Council of Baltimore.[3] And it quotes once more, from previous documents, the displeasure expressed by the Supreme Pontiff in this matter: *"sibi minime placere, atque eliminandam prorsus,"* stating that this phrase was even incorporated in the 397th Baltimore Decree.[4]

The Holy See had hoped that, after all the aforementioned repudiations, the custom would surely be stopped everywhere. Yet, since truthworthy information recently reached Rome that the condemned practice still flourished in some places, the present admonition was deemed appropriate by the Sacred Congregation.

The letter expresses a surprisingly thorough knowledge of the

[1] *II Juris Pontificii,* MXCVII, pp. 686-687; *Coll. Lac.,* III, 1085c-1086b.

[2] Cf. *supra,* p. 40.

[3] Cf. *supra,* pp. 50, 51.

[4] Cf. *supra,* p. 51.

abuse. It covers so many aspects of the problem and is so carefully yet elegantly worded that much would be lost were it not quoted, at least in part, in the present treatise.

Abbreviated versions of this Admonition have been reprinted in various places.[5] The following translation, however, was made by the writer from the original document, as quoted in the *Juris Pontificii* Collection compiled by R. De Martinis (1829-1900).

> [It was hoped, after all the previous repudiations, that the practice of demanding money at the door of the church would cease.] . . . However, the Sacred Congregation has learned, from the recent reports of many who are worthy of belief, what has really taken place—something which it was least expecting, and which it received not without great surprise. Indeed, it has information that in certain churches of the United States the aforesaid practice continues as before; in some churches not outside, but within the doors, immediately upon their entry, money is demanded from the faithful as they come into the church; in other churches, the poor among the faithful are by no means turned away from entering if they have no money to contribute, but they are compelled on account of their poverty to stand thus exposed and humiliated before all, to their great embarrassment; so much so, that sometimes many stay away from hearing Mass. Since this Sacred Congregation first learned these things, it has not ceased to alert the solicitude of certain bishops against the aforesaid abuses, by special letters. Moreover, since these warnings seemed to have been given in vain, and since it is sufficiently clear that this previously mentioned practice has exposed the Catholic name many times to the jokes and reproaches of the heretics, the Sacred Congregation, in desiring to abolish and eliminate it entirely, does not now cease to exhort Your Excellency in the Lord, if by chance you should know that a custom of this sort is gaining strength in various places in your diocese, that you should put forth every effort to see to it that when the faithful enter churches in order to be present at the divine mysteries or to hear the word of God, that likewise there be no collectors whatsoever placed at the doors of these same churches. Through this, however, the Sacred Congregation by no means intends to forbid the offering of money volun-

[5] *Collectanea S. Congregationis de Propaganda Fide* (2 vols., Romae: Typographia Polyglotta S. C. de Propaganda Fide, 1907), II, n. 1345; *Fontes*, n. 4875.

> tarily made by the faithful at the Offertory, as is the custom up to the present time in a great number of churches in the United States. This Sacred Congregation certainly feels that all prelates and rectors of churches will conform to this regulation without any delay whatsoever. But if it should happen otherwise, against our hope, as we are sorry to say has happened up to the present, then there will have to be prepared, although unwillingly, more stringent measures against the transgressors. Finally, I am not forgetting to notify Your Excellency that everything which has been related above was reported to our Holy Father, Pope Pius IX, in an audience of the sixth of June of the present year, and all the suggested remedial means were approved by His Holiness. . . .

The document certainly speaks for itself, so that for the immediate purpose at hand no further comment appears to be necessary. In fact, after a reading of the aforesaid letter, anything more—beyond a reiteration that the practice of collecting money at the church door, in any manner whatsoever, was completely and unconditionally repudiated—would seem superfluous.

CHAPTER VII

PARTICULAR LEGISLATION

ARTICLE 1. THE THIRD PLENARY COUNCIL OF BALTIMORE

In an Apostolic letter dated January 1, 1884, Pope Leo XIII selected the city of Baltimore as the site for the III Plenary Council of Baltimore, and he appointed Archbishop James Gibbons (1834-1921) as the presiding officer and Apostolic Legate of the assembly. The Council was opened Sunday, November 9, 1884, and its last Solemn Session was held on December 7, of the same year.

The Decrees of this Council as promulgated—like those of the I and II Plenary Councils—were applicable to the entire United States. (Between the II and III Plenary Councils of Baltimore, the Sacred Congregation for the Propagation of the Faith issued the official Admonition which has been treated previously.) [1]

The III Plenary Council, in its 288th official Decree, again condemned the practice of exacting money at the door of the church, calling to mind the previous prohibitions by Pope Pius IX and the II Plenary Council, and it demanded that the custom be everywhere abolished. The statute itself is worded thus:

> Praxis, sicubi forte existat, pecuniam exigendi ad fores ecclesiae Dominicis ac Festis diebus, ut quis ingredi possit ac sacrosancto missae sacrificio interesse, jampridem eliminari debuisset. Eam enim damnavit Summus Pontifex Pius IX. et prorsus tollendam significavit. Decessores quoque nostri supremo ejus judicio obsequentes finem pravae huic consuetudini omnino imponendum esse statuerunt. (Conc. Plen. Balt. II., No. 397.) [2]

In the following decree the Council legislated concerning the rent-free pews which every church must provide for the accommodation of the poor.[3]

[1] Cf. *supra,* Chapter VI, pp. 52-54.

[2] *III Plen. Conc. Balt.,* Titulus IX, Caput V., Num. 288.

[3] Cf. *supra,* pp. 23-27, where the implications of this statute are treated.

> In unaquaque ecclesia constituatur spatium liberum ubi fideles Sacro adesse et verbum Dei audire possint. In hoc autem spatio eligendo et in eorum usum aptando, nunquam obliviscatur ille, qui ecclesiae praeest, hos homines esse Christi pauperes, et Boni Pastoris exemplo misericorditer cum illis agat, seduloque vitet quidquid eos contemnendi aut pudefaciendi specimen prae se ferre possit. Secus enim, (quod Apostolus expresse vetat) exhonorantur pauperes (Jac. II. 2-6), et timeri aliquando potest ne per pastorem ecclesiae ii, pro quorum aeque ac pro divitum animabus rationem est redditurus, a divino cultu et a vita Christiana penitus arceantur.[4]

Article 2. Archdiocesan and Diocesan Synods

Section 1. Synodal Treatment of Door Collections

After its repeated condemnations had been made known, various Archdiocesan and Diocesan Synods, as well as Provincial Councils, which were held in the United States began to include among their statutes a specific prohibition against the practice of demanding money at the door of the church.

The fact that many dioceses had no such particular law against this practice seems to indicate that no abuse was current in those areas. Yet, on the other hand, it must not be concluded that the abuse had flourished in all those places where a synodal prohibition *was* written into the law. Such legislation might well have the effect of a preventive norm, in place of being simply a corrective measure.

The earlier synodal laws (particularly those of the last century and up to the advent of the Code of Canon Law) are of special interest, because they reflect, even in their wording, the impact of the Plenary Councils of Baltimore and the repeated emphasis placed by the Sacred Congregation for the Propagation of the Faith on doing away with this practice "immediately" and in all its forms. Moreover, these early synods provide an insight into the general tone of the law as it existed on the local level before 1918, when the Code of Canon Law went into effect.

For almost four centuries prior to the Vatican Council, which convened in 1869, the Church had no complete and exclusive

[4] *III Plen. Conc. Balt.*, Titulus IX, Caput V, Num. 289.

authentic collection of its laws. Such a compilation was urged by the hierarchy at that Council; but, because the city of Rome was occupied by Italian troops in 1870, the Council adjourned without taking action on the proposal.

This great task was eventually begun under the authority of Pope Pius X in 1904. On May 27, 1917, the completed Code of Canon Law was officially promulgated by Pope Benedict XV through his Apostolic Constitution *Providentissima Mater Ecclesia;* it was to become effective on the Feast of Pentecost, May 19, 1918.

It may be said, in brief, that the Code represented a complete, authentic, and exclusive collection of the universal law prevailing throughout the Church at the time of its promulgation, apart from the special norms and regulations issued for the Oriental Church.

Gratuitous access to the church for sacred rites was treated under Title IX in Book III of the Code. The law itself, as promulgated in canon 1181, was one of the very few in the Code which include in their make-up a specific reprobation of all contrary customs.

By 1918, it is safe to assume, the abuse of door collections had become more extensive. Faced with the existence or possible encroachment of a custom which was expressly repudiated by the universal law of the Church, many dioceses saw fit to draw special attention to the law in question by reiterating it among their subsequent synodal decrees.

Section 2. Competence of the Diocesan Synod to Urge Observance of the Universal Law

A synod is an assembly or gathering of the clergy of a diocese convoked by the bishop for the purpose of considering matters related to the particular necessity or welfare of the clergy and the laity.[5]

It is urged by many that the archdiocesan or diocesan synod should not include among its statutes a repetition of the universal laws of the Church. According to the norms of the Code itself, this is certainly a justifiable opinion. Universal laws oblige all

[5] Cf. can. 356, § 1.

for whom they are given, everywhere;[6] and since all are presumed to know the law unless the contrary is proved,[7] little or nothing would seem to be gained through a repetition among the diocesan synodal statutes of these same universal laws already effectively in force.

Donnelly, in his dissertation on the diocesan synod, makes the following observation:

> . . . since the statutes [of a synod] are intended to be supplementary to the Code, to contain what the Code has not provided for, it is preferable not to incorporate its canons in the statutes. In fact, if the canons of the Code are not heeded it is not likely that greater attention will be given them as statutes. . . . The only means to be taken to promote a better observance of the general law in the diocese by synodal statutes is, if urgently necessary, to enact penal sanctions.[8]

Much may be said in favor of this opinion. The policy of "stuffing" the decrees of a synod with a constant repetition of the universal law, when there is no specific need for such a repetition, is certainly to be discouraged. If, however, a certain universal law of the Church is being violated in a given area, it seems to be the duty of the bishop to call attention to the law itself and to take measures to suppress any abuses which may be arising.

In virtue of his office, the bishop of the diocese must urge the observance of the laws of the Church.[9] Moreover, he has the duty to guard ecclesiastical discipline against abuses, especially in regard to the administration of the sacraments and the sacramentals, the worship of God and the veneration of the saints, the preaching of the word of God, indulgences, and care for the exact execution of pious wills.[10]

Although he is not in favor of incorporating the universal laws

[6] Can. 13, § 1.

[7] Cf. can. 16, § 2.

[8] Donnelly, *The Diocesan Synod,* The Catholic University of America Canon Law Studies, No. 74 (Washington, D. C.: The Catholic University of America, 1932), p. 89.

[9] Can. 336, § 1.

[10] Cf. can. 336, § 2.

in a diocesan synod, Donnelly holds that the bishop may use the occasion of a synod to *speak* to the clergy concerning the laws which are being disregarded.

> More particularly the competence of the synod may be divided as follows: (1) it can urge that the law of the Code be better observed; it can determine more definitely matter treated only substantially by the Code. . . . A bishop is obliged to this vigilance [regarding the exact observance of the universal law] by reason of his pastoral office. The synod offers an excellent opportunity to attend to the obligation most effectively. . . . A bishop may use the occasion of a synod to speak to the assembled clergy of the disregarded laws. But, since the statutes are intended to be supplementary to the Code, to contain what the Code has not provided for, it is preferable not to incorporate its canons in the statutes.[11]

If, however, the violation in question is widespread, it seems reasonable that, after speaking to the clergy about the matter, the most effective means of stressing the observance of the law would be to call attention to it in the diocesan synodal decrees, and to demand conformity on the part of all.

Section 3. A Synodal Survey

In order to obtain a comprehensive picture of particular legislation as it has existed in this country relative to the matter of door collections, a survey was conducted by the writer in the fall of 1956, in the form of a letter sent to most of the archdiocesan and diocesan chanceries. Ninety-nine replies were received out of a total of one hundred and twenty-six questionnaires sent out. The kindness of the Most Reverend Bishops and the Very Reverend Chancellors, in responding, thus permits the results of the survey to represent seventy-nine per cent of the chanceries questioned.

The primary object was to establish whether or not individual archdioceses or dioceses have dealt with the matter of canon 1181 by means of synodal legislation. Comments and suggestions were also requested, and the ones received proved most helpful to the writer in the course of preparing the dissertation.

[11] Donnelly, *The Diocesan Synod*, pp. 88-89.

Following, then, is a chart which utilizes the survey responses and the available copies of various synods to indicate whether or not the archdioceses and dioceses in this country have ever promulgated particular laws prohibiting collections at the door of the church.

It should be noted that in many of the older dioceses the bishops instituted legislation prohibiting door collections in some of the earlier synods, but that in the more recent synods the bishops make no mention of such a prohibition. In other dioceses, the procedure has been exactly the reverse.

It must be borne in mind, therefore, that a check mark under the "Synodal legislation" column does not necessarily refer to the statutes of the most recent synod of the archdiocese or diocese in question.

Perhaps it should be repeated here that one must not conclude that the abuse of door collections existed in all those places where a synodal prohibition was written into the law. Such legislation could easily serve as a preventive norm as well as a corrective measure.

SYNODAL LEGISLATION CHART

KEY

Yes——Synodal Legislation at some time or other regarding the matter of canon 1181.

No——No such Synodal Legislation promulgated insofar as the writer was able to determine.

Other—No Synodal Legislation against door collections proper to the diocese itself, but an obligation in the matter deriving from provincial law or from the temporarily appropriated synodal legislation of another diocese.

Archdiocese	*Yes*	*No*	*Other*
Baltimore	X		
Boston	X		
Chicago	X		
Cincinnati	X		
Denver	X		
Detroit		X	
Dubuque	X		
Hartford	X		
Indianapolis	X		
Kansas City in Kansas	X		
Los Angeles	X		
Louisville		X	
Milwaukee		X	
Newark	X		
New Orleans		X	
New York	X		
Omaha	X		

Archdiocese	*Yes*	*No*	*Other*
Philadelphia	X		
Portland in Oregon	X		
St. Louis	X		
St. Paul		X	
San Antonio		X	
San Francisco	X		
Santa Fe	X		
Seattle	X		
Washington		X	

Diocese	*Yes*	*No*	*Other*
Albany	X		
Alexandria		X	
Altoona-Johnstown	X		
Amarillo		X	
Atlanta	X		
Baker			X
Bellevelle	X		
Bismarck	X		
Boise			X
Bridgeport			X
Brooklyn	X		
Buffalo	X		
Burlington		X	
Camden	X		
Charleston		X	
Cheyenne		X	
Cleveland	X		
Columbus	X		
Corpus Christi		X	
Covington		X	
Crookston	X		
Dallas-Fort Worth		X	
Davenport		X	
Des Moines	X		
Dodge City (*Pro-Synodal Decree*)	X		
Duluth	X		
El Paso		X	
Erie		X	
Evansville	X		
Fall River	X		
Fargo	X		
Fort Wayne-South Bend	X		
Gallup		X	
Galveston-Houston	X		
Grand Rapids	X		
Great Falls		X	
Green Bay	X		
Greensburg			X
Harrisburg	X		
Helena			X
Honolulu		X	
Joliet		X	
Juneau		X	
Kansas City-St. Joseph	X		
La Crosse	X		
Lafayette (Louisiana)	X		
Lafayette in Indiana		X	
Lansing		X	
Lincoln		X	
Little Rock		X	
Madison	X		
Manchester	X		
Marquette		X	
Mobile-Birmingham	X		
Monterey-Fresno	X		
Nashville	X		
Natchez-Jackson		X	
Ogdensburg		X	
Oklahoma City and Tulsa	X		
Owensboro		X	
Peoria	X		
Pittsburgh	X		
Portland		X	
Providence	X		
Pueblo		X	
Raleigh	X		
Rapid City		X	
Reno		X	
Richmond		X	
Rochester	X		
Rockford		X	

Diocese	*Yes*	*No*	*Other*	*Diocese*	*Yes*	*No*	*Other*
Sacramento		X		Springfield-in-Illinois	X		
Saginaw		X		Steubenville		X	
St. Augustine		X		Superior	X		
St. Cloud		X		Syracuse	X		
Salina		X		Toledo	X		
Salt Lake City	X			Trenton	X		
San Diego	X			Tucson		X	
Savannah	X			Wheeling	X		
Scranton	X			Wichita		X	
Sioux City	X			Wilmington	X		
Sioux Falls		X		Winona		X	
Spokane		X		Worcester		X	
Springfield (Massachusetts)		X		Yakima			X
				Youngstown		X	

Section 4. Various Synodal Laws

Herein are contained a few of the statutes, drawn from archdiocesan and diocesan synods held in this country, which prohibit collections from being taken up at the church doors. The arrangement is alphabetical, and the archdiocesan legislation is given first consideration.

No atempt has been made to include all archdioceses and dioceses which have had synodal legislation concerning this matter or to cite all of the synods held in any particular place. Obviously, such a task would be beyond the scope of the present work.

The places chosen, however, are fairly representative of all parts of the country, and the synodal dates span a great many years. Statutes from many synods were found to contain identical or similar wording. An attempt was generally made to avoid repetition and to select as many differently worded prohibitions as possible.

The microfilm library at the Catholic University of America, available copies of various synods, and the archdioceses and dioceses throughout the country provided the writer with most of the information from which the following statutes are cited.

The reader is referred to the Bibliography for a more comprehensive listing of synods held in this country.

THE ARCHDIOCESE OF BOSTON

(Erected April 8, 1808; Created an Archdiocese in 1875.)

I Synod (August 21, 1842):

> Penitus prohibemus ne unquam in hac nostra dioecesi, quacumque de causa etiam pia, a fidelibus exigatur ut ad portas ecclesiae pecuniam solvant, aut chartulas pecunia emptas exhibeant, antequam ipsis pateat ad missam aut ad alia divini cultus officia introitus. Consuetudinem etiam illam quae nonnullis in locis viget, collocandi intra sanctuarium festis diebus Nativitatis Dominicae et Paschae mensam ut fideles accedentes pecunias, quas oblationes vocant, super eam deponant, abrogamus ac prohibemus, cum timendum sit ne scandalum inde enascatur. Haec autem statuendo nullo modo cohibere intendimus laudabilem illam fidelium pietatem qua solent hisce in festis aut quovis alio tempore, sustentationi suorum pastorum, pecuniis vel aliis rebus oblatis, subvenire; modo tamen omnis scandali occasio amoveatur.[12]

II Synod (November 5, 1868):

> Penitus prohibemus ne unquam in hac Nostra Dioecesi quacumque de causa a fidelibus exigatur ut ad portas ecclesiae pecuniam solvant, aut chartulas pecunia emptas exhibeant, antequam ipsis pateat ad sacrum aedificium ingressus. *Conc. Plen. n. 397. Syn. Bost. I. n. 18.*[13]

Synod of 1886:

This Synod restated verbatim the prohibition contained in the II Synod, and added, in the same statute, the following:

> Imo in unaquaque ecclesia constituatur spatium liberum, ubi fideles pretium sedis solvere aut non valentes aut nolentes, Sacro adesse et verbum Dei audire possint. *Conc. Plen. II, n. 397; Conc. Plen. III. nn. 288, 289. Syn. Bost. I. n. 18.*[14]

12 *Synodus Dioecesana, Bostoniensis I, 21 aug. 1842* (Bostoniae: Ex Typis Patritii Donahoe [no date given]), Num. XVIII.

13 *Constitutiones Dioecesanae . . . in Synodo Dioecesana Secunda . . . Latae et Promulgatae, 5 nov. 1868* [no place or date of publication given], Titulus XIV, Num. 178.

14 *Constitutiones Dioecesanae . . . Latae et Promulgatae, anno 1886* (Bostoniae, 1886), Titulus XV, Num. 209.

VI Synod (April 7, 1919):

Repeated verbatim the first sentence of Statute 18 of the I Synod. This sentence alone constituted the only pertinent legislation of the VI Synod.[15]

VII Synod (May 29, 1952):

> Entrance to the church for sacred functions must at all times be absolutely free and without charge. There shall be no signs or other indications that a fixed offering is required. Neither the parish priest, the assistants, nor the ushers shall by word or expression show objection if an offering is not given.[16]

THE ARCHDIOCESE OF CHICAGO

(Established November 28, 1843; Created an Archdiocese in 1880.)

I Synod (December 13, 1887):

> Monitis Conciliorum Plenariorum Baltimorensium II. et III. obsequentes, omnino prohibemus ne pecunia ad fores ecclesiae exigatur, ut ecclesiam intrare divinisque mysteriis adstare fidelis quivis possit. Imo stricte praecipimus ut in unaquaque ecclesia constituatur spatium liberum, ubi pretium sedis solvere aut non valentes aut nolentes, Sacro interesse et verbum Dei audire possint. (*Conc. Plen. II. 397; III. 288, 289.*) [17]

III Synod (December 14, 1905):

Repeated verbatim the wording of the I Synod.[18]

[15] *Constitutiones Dioeceseos Bostoniensis Quae in Synodo Dioecesana Sexta . . . Latae et Promulgatae Fuerunt, 7 april. 1919* (Bostoniae: Ex Typis "Washington Press," 1919), Titulus XV, Num. 187.

[16] *Acta et Statuta Synodi Bostoniensis Septimae, 29 maii. 1952* [no place or date of publication given], Title XVII, No. 166.

[17] *Synodus Dioecesana Chicagiensis Prima, 13 dec. 1887* (Chicagiae: Ex Typis Cameron, Amberg et Sociorum, 1887), Titulus XX, Num. 253.

[18] *Synodus Dioecesana Chicagiensis . . . Tertia, 14 dec. 1905* (Chicagine: Typis Mandarunt Cameron, Amberg Sociique, 1906), Titulus XX, Num. 268.

THE ARCHDIOCESE OF CINCINNATI

(Established June 19, 1821; Created an Archdiocese July 19, 1850.)

V Synod (December 14, 1954):

Admission to the church and to divine services must always be free and without any charge or collection required at the entrance or in the vestibule (cf. can. 1181, s. 226).[19]

It is permissible to collect seat money during Mass, as long as proper decorum is observed (cf. s. 139).[20]

THE ARCHDIOCESE OF NEWARK

(Established in 1853; Erected an Archdiocese December 10, 1937.)

I Archdiocesan Synod (June 3, 1941):

Admission to the church for divine services must be absolutely free. (Canon 1181) Hence We strictly forbid in this Archdiocese that a fee be charged or tickets previously bought be demanded from the faithful before they are allowed to enter the church for any divine service.[21]

THE ARCHDIOCESE OF OMAHA

(Established as a Vicariate Apostolic January 6, 1857; Erected a Diocese October 2, 1885; Created an Archdiocese August 7, 1945.)

IV Synod (June 14, 1934):

In pecuniis colligendis omnino et religiose abstinendum est a qualibet specie indecentiae vel scandali periculo; qua de causa strictissime observandas esse mandamus sequentes regulas:

19 *Fifth Synod of the Archdiocese of Cincinnati, December 14, 1954* [no place or date of publication given], Section IV, No. 139.

20 *Ibid.*, Section VII, No. 226.

21 *Statutes of the Archdiocese of Newark enacted and promulgated . . . in the First Archdiocesan Synod (Sixteenth of the Diocese of Newark), June 3, 1941* (Arlington, N. J.: Catholic Protectory Press, 1941), No. 205.

1°. Sub poenis gravissimis infligendis, non excepta suspensione, prohibemus, quominus sacerdos sub quolibet praetextu intra Missam ab altari recedat, aedemque sacram circumeat, ut a fidelibus petat eleemosynas. (*Conc. Plen. Balt. III, n. 293.*)

2°. "Ingressus in ecclesiam ad sacros ritus sit omnino gratuitus, reprobata qualibet contraria consuetudine" (Can. 1181). Deinde nequit tolerari consuetudo exigendi pecunias ad foras ecclesiae diebus dominicis aut festivis, antequam quis ad Missam audiendam ingredi possit. Licet tamen intra Missam per laicos collectas habere ad percipiendos reditus pro locatione scamnorum modo tamen decenti et a qualibet molestia personali libero.

3°. Sine licentia Ordinarii ne fiant collectae in ecclesia pro quolibet opere, quod ad bonum paroeciae directe non referatur.[22]

THE ARCHDIOCESE OF PHILADELPHIA

(*Established in 1808; Created an Archdiocese February 12, 1875.*)

IX Synod (April 26, 1934):

It is strictly forbidden to ask or receive money at or near a church door either for entrance into the church; or as an offering or payment for a seat in it.[23]

THE ARCHDIOCESE OF PORTLAND IN OREGON

(*Erected as a Vicariate Apostolic December 1, 1843; Created the Archdiocese of Oregon City July 24, 1846; Redesignated the Archdiocese of Portland in Oregon September 26, 1928.*)

IV Provincial Council (September 8-10, 1932):

§ 1. Omnino prohibetur quominus sacerdotes sive saeculares sive religiosi per se vel per alios pecuniam colligant ad ingressum ecclesiae vel scamnorum et sedium.

[22] *Synodus Dioecesana Omahensis Quarta, 14 iun. 1934* (Omaha in Statu Nebraska: Typis Burkley Envelope & Printing Company, 1934), Caput XXXII, Num. 392, 1°, 2°, 3°.

[23] *Synodus Dioecesana Philadelphiensis IX, 26 april. 1934* [no place or date of publication given], Num. XLV.

§ 2. Permittuntur tantum voluntariae collectiones infra sacra.[24]

THE ARCHDIOCESE OF ST. LOUIS

(Established a Diocese July 14, 1826; Created an Archdiocese July 20, 1847.)

VII Synod (June 10, 1929):

Ab introeuntibus ecclesiam ad Divina audienda pecuniam expetendi praxis est prorsus reprobanda.[25]

VIII Synod (May 10, 1950):

Admission to the church for sacred functions must be absolutely free of charge; no money may be taken at the entrance of the church. We forbid any action or custom to the contrary. (Cf. Canon 1181.) [26]

THE ARCHDIOCESE OF SAN FRANCISCO

(Established July 29, 1853.)

II Synod (October 14, 1936):

In pecuniis colligendis omnino et religiose abstinendum est a qualibet specie indecentiae vel scandali periculo; qua de cause strictissime observandas esse mandamus sequentes regulas: . . .

2°."Ingressus in ecclesiam ad sacros ritus sit omnino gratuitus, reprobata qualibet contraria consuetudine" (Can. 1181). Deinde nequit tolerari consuetudo exigendi pecunias ad foras ecclesiae diebus dominicis aut festivis, antequam quis ad Missam audiendam ingredi possit. Licet tamen intra Missam per laicos collectas habere ad percipiendos reditus pro

[24] *Acta et Decreta Concilii Provincialis Portlandensis in Oregon Quarti, 8-10 sept. 1932* (Portland, Oregon: Sentinel Printery, 1934), Pars Quinta, Titulus I, Decretum 357, § 1, § 2.

[25] *Synodus Dioecesana Sancti Ludovici Septima, 10 iun. 1929* (Sancti Ludovici: Apud Cancellariam Dioecesanam [no date given]), Caput "De Locis et Temporibus Sacris," Num. 113.

[26] *Synodus Dioecesana Sancti Ludovici Octava, 10 maii. 1950* [no place or date of publication given], Chapter III, Section II, Title 1, No. 82.

locatione scamnorum, modo tamen decenti et a qualibet molestia personali libero.[27]

THE DIOCESE OF ALBANY

(*Established April 23, 1847.*)

III Synod (February 6-7, 1884):

Concilii Balt. Plen. II. monitis obsequentes, omnino prohibemus, ne ad fores ecclesiae pecunia exigatur, ut Templum Dei intrare, divinisque mysteriis adstare quis possit. Consuetudini hujusmodi, sicubi existat, volumus ut finis continuo ponatur.[28]

The following synods contain a verbatim or similarly worded prohibition:

IV Synod (July 19, 1887) [29]

V Synod (December 2, 1890) [30]

VI Synod (January 31, 1895) [31]

The following two synods promulgated again the decrees of the previous synods, inaugurated a few changes and additions, but made no special reference to door collections:

27 *Statuta Archidioecesis Sancti Francisci Lata ac Promulgata . . . in Synodo Dioecesana Secunda, 14 oct. 1936* (San Francisco, California: Typis: The Monitor Publishing Company [no date given]), Titulus V, Caput III, Decretum 380, 2°.

28 *Synodus Dioecesana Albanensis Tertia, 6-7 febr. 1884* (Neo-Eboraci: Typis "Catholic Publication Society Co.," 1884), Caput Decimum Septimum, Num. 143.

29 *Synodus Dioecesana Albanensis Quarta, Synodus Superiores Mutans et Agens, 19 iul. 1887* (Trojae: Excudebat T. J. Hurley, 1887), Num. 143.

30 *Synodus Dioecesana Albanensis Quinta, 2 dec. 1890* (Trojae: Excudebat T. J. Hurley, 1890), Num. 160.

31 *Statuta Dioecesis Albanensis in Sexta Synodo Dioecesana . . . Promulgata et Edita, 31 ian. 1895* (Albaniae: Excudebant Weed-Parsons Sociique, Typographi, 1895), Num. 159.

VII Synod (January 4, 1898) [32]

VIII Synod (January 16, 1901) [33]

THE DIOCESE OF ALTOONA-JOHNSTOWN

(Established as the Diocese of Altoona May 30, 1901; Redesignated the Diocese of Altoona-Johnstown October 9, 1957.)

I Synod (November 29, 1922):

Prorsus abhorreant omnes hujus dioecesis sacerdotes a prava illa consuetudine, qua Dominicis et Festis diebus pecunia exigatur ut quis ecclesiam ingredi ac sacrosancto Missae sacrificio interesse possit.[34]

THE DIOCESE OF BELLEVILLE

(Established January 7, 1887.)

II Synod (June 15, 1904):

Ad fores ecclesiae Dominicis et festis diebus pecuniam exigere, ut quis ingredi possit, omnino prohibetur.[35]

III Synod (November 19, 1909):

Ad fores ecclesiae diebus dominicis et festis pecuniam exigere, ut quis ingredi possit, omnino prohibitum est, et quidem sub quocunque praetextu.[36]

32 *Statuta Dioecesis Albanensis in Septima Synodo Dioecesana . . . Promulgata et Edita, 4 ian. 1898* (Albaniae: Excudebant Weed-Parsons Sociique, Typographi, 1898).

33 *Statuta Dioecesis Albanensis in Octava Synodo Dioecesana . . . Promulgata et Edita, 16 ian. 1901* (Albaniae: Excudebant Weed-Parsons Sociique, Typographi, 1901).

34 *Synodus Altunensis Prima, 29 nov. 1922* (Lancaster, Pa.: Wickersham Printing Co., 1923), Caput 15, Num. 143.

35 *Synodus Dioecesana Bellevillensis Secunda, 15 iun. 1904* (Belleville, Illinois: Buechler Printing Company [no date given]), Titulus "De Modis Prohibitis Pecunias Colligendi," Num. 1.

36 *Synodus Dioecesana Bellevillensis Tertia, 19 nov. 1909* (Belleville, Illinois: Buechler Printing Company, 1909), Titulus "De Modis Prohibitis Pecunias Colligendi," Num. 1.

The following synods contain a prohibition which is almost verbatim:

IV Synod (December 1, 1920) [37]

V Synod (December 27, 1939) [38]

THE DIOCESE OF BISMARCK

(*Established December 31, 1909.*)

I Synod (November 12, 1924):

> Canon 1181 commands: "Admission to divine service must be entirely free and every contrary custom is hereby reprobated." Pew rent is hereby not forbidden, neither soliciting for a contribution from those who have no pew; but free admission to the house of God must be accorded to every Catholic, even the poorest.[39]

THE DIOCESE OF BROOKLYN

(*Established in 1853.*)

I Synod (August 29, 1879):

> Monitis porro Concilii Plen. Baltim. II. obsequentes, omnino prohibemus ne pecunia ad fores ecclesiae exigatur ut ecclesiam intrare divinisque mysteriis adstare fidelis quisque possit. Consuetudini hujusmodi, sicubi existat, volumus ut finis continuo ponatur.[40]

[37] *Synodus Dioecesana Bellevillensis Quarta, 1 dec. 1920* (Belleville, Ill.: Buechler Printing Co. [no date given]), Titulus "De Modis Prohibitis Pecunias Colligendi," Num. 1.

[38] *Statuta Dioecesis Bellevillensis Lata ac Promulgata . . . in Synodo Dioecesana Bellevillensi Quinta, 27 dec. 1939* (Belleville, Illinois: Buechler Printing Co., 1940), Titulus "De Modis Prohibitis Pecunias Colligendi," Num. 269.

[39] *First Diocesan Synod of the Diocese of Bismarck, Nov. 12, 1924* [no place or date of publication given], Part II, Chapter X, Section "A," No. 1.

[40] *Statuta Synodi Brooklynensis* [sic] *Primae, 29 aug. 1879* (Neo-Eboraci: Ex Typis H. J. Hewitt, 1880), Titulus "De Pastoribus," Caput Tertium, Num. XII.

The following synods contain a similarly worded prohibition:

III Synod (December 27, 1894) [41]

V Synod (February 25-26, 1926) [42]

THE DIOCESE OF BUFFALO

(Established April 23, 1847.)

XXVIII Synod (November 9, 1938):

DOOR COLLECTIONS: No collection may be made at the doors of a church, under any pretext whatever.[43]

THE DIOCESE OF CAMDEN

(Established December 9, 1937.)

I Synod (May 17, 1955):

Districte interdicitur ne pecunia petatur, neve accipiatur, sive ad valvas, sive prope valvas ecclesiae, seu pro ingressu in ecclesiam uti taxa pro sede.[44]

THE DIOCESE OF CLEVELAND

(Established April 23, 1847.)

VI Synod (May 23-26, 1882):

Door collections are not allowed in any church in this Diocese. Where pews are not rented, and the income is raised

41 *Constitutiones Dioecesanae Brooklynienses* [sic] *quas in Synodo Dioecesana Tertia . . . Sanxit et Promulgavit, 27 dec. 1894* (Neo-Eboraci: Typis Missionis Virginis Immaculatae, 1895), Titulus XX, Num. 272.

42 *Constitutiones Dioecesanae Brooklynienses* [sic] *quas in Synodo Dioecesana Quinta . . . Sanxit et Promulgavit, 25-26 febr. 1926* (New York: Press of Loughlin Bros. [no date given]), Titulus XX, Num. 273.

43 *Synodus Dioecesana Buffalensis Duodetricesima, 9 nov. 1938* (Buffalo: Union and Times Press [no date given]), Art. 125.

44 *Synodus Dioecesana Camdensis Prima, 17 maii. 1955* (Philadelphia, Pa.: Press of Jefferies and Manz, Inc. [no date given]), Pars II, Caput VII, Num. 222.

by voluntary contributions, collections shall be taken in the pews only, but never at the door or by collectors standing at the foot of the aisle.[45]

THE DIOCESE OF COLUMBUS

(*Established in 1868.*)

V Synod (October 8, 1952):

It is strictly forbidden to collect money at the door, in the entrances or vestibule of the church. An exception is made for missionaries who have permission of the Ordinary, and for collectors for the poor (Saint Vincent de Paul Society) who have the permission of the pastor.[46]

THE DIOCESE OF CROOKSTON

(*Established December 31, 1909.*)

Synod of September 20, 1921:

Admission to divine services must be entirely free and every contrary custom is hereby reprobated. (Can. 1181.)

We, therefore, order pastors to see to it that no one demands anything in money or tickets previously sold, at the church door. As this church regulation, however, does not forbid the solicitation of an offering from persons who have no pew, and wish to occupy one, the ushers will show such persons to a pew, in a gentlemanly way, and collect the contribution during service. The privilege of free admission to the house of God must be accorded, without discrimination, to every man, woman and child, even the poorest.[47]

[45] *Acta* [*et Statuta*] *Synodi Dioecesanae Clevelandensis Sextae, 23-26 maii. 1882* (contained in *Statuta Dioecesis Clevelandensis, in Synodis Dioecesanis, Habitis Annis Domini 1852, 1854, 1857, 1868, 1872, 1882, Lata et, prout nunc Prostant, Edita in Synodo, die 27 mensis Maii, A.D. 1882* [Clevelandi: M. E. M'Cabe, Typographus, 1882]), Num. 205.

[46] *Fifth Synod of the Diocese of Columbus, October 8, 1952* [no place or date of publication given], Chapter IX, Statute No. 110.

[47] *Statutes of the Diocese of Crookston Promulgated at the Diocesan Synod held September 20, 1921* (St. Louis, Mo.: B. Herder Book Co., 1923), Chapter VII, Par. 2, No. 348.

THE DIOCESE OF DES MOINES

(Erected August 12, 1911.)

Synod of June 15, 1923:

Admission to divine services must be entirely free, and no one may be debarred or embarrassed by the collection of fees, and the poor must be always well provided for. But this does not mean that those who wish a seat or a kneeler and who can pay for them, may not be expected to do so. We shall bless the day when this can be discontinued, and the pastor who will devise a means of maintaining the church from without, so that entrance and all comforts may be entirely free to all, will receive a special ray of glory. Can. 1181.[48]

THE DIOCESE OF DODGE CITY

(Established May 19, 1951.)

Diocesan Statutes promulgated September 12, 1952:

Admission to the church for sacred functions must be absolutely free of charge. (Cf. Canon 1181.) [49]

THE DIOCESE OF EVANSVILLE

(Established November 11, 1944.)

I Synod (October 11, 1948):

Admission to the sacred functions in the church must be absolutely free of charge. We forbid any action or custom to the contrary, such as collecting seat money at the church doors on Sundays and Holy Days. (Cf. Canon 1181.) [50]

48 *The Code of the Diocese of Des Moines Decreed in Diocesan Synod held June 15th, 1923* [no place or date of publication given], Section III, Chapter III, No. 250.

49 Cf. *The Statutes of the Diocese of Dodge City,* as promulgated by His Excellency, the Most Reverend John B. Franz, Bishop of Dodge City, in the Pro-Synodal Decree of September 12, 1952.

50 *Statuta Dioecesis Evansvicensis Lata ac Promulgata . . . in Synodo Dioecesana Prima, 11 oct. 1948* (Evansville, Ind.: Typis: Moser Printing Co. [no date given]), Pars III, Sectio II, Titulus I, Statutum 85, n. 3.

THE DIOCESE OF FALL RIVER

(*Established March 12, 1904.*)

I Synod (June 28, 1905):

Praxis pecuniam exigendi ad fores ecclesiae, ut quis ingredi ac Sacrosancto Missae Sacrificio interesse possit, omnino damnanda est et prorsus eliminanda.—Conc. Plen. Balt. III, 288.[51]

In unaquaque ecclesia spatium liberum constituatur in quo fideles taxam pro sede solvere non valentes, aut etiam nolentes, Missae Sacrificio interesse et verbum Dei audire queant.[52]

THE DIOCESE OF FARGO

(*Established November 12, 1889.*)

I Synod (September 29-30, 1941):

1. Omnino prohibetur quominus sacerdotes, sive saeculares sive religiosi, per se vel per alios, ad ingressum ecclesiae pecuniam colligant.
2. Oblationes voluntariae infra sacra, prout de more, solummodo permittuntur.[53]

II Synod (October 2-3, 1951):

The wording of the I Synod is repeated verbatim.[54]

[51] *Statuta Dioecesis Riverormensis Quae in Synodo Dioecesana Prima . . . Sanxit et Promulgavit, 28 iun. 1905* (Philadelphia: Ex Typis The Dolphin Press, 1905), Caput XVII, Num. 177.

[52] *Ibid.*, Num. 178.

[53] *Synodus Dioecesana Fargensis Prima, 29-30 sept. 1941* (Milwauchiae: Ex Typographia Bruce, 1941), Pars Prima, Titulus Septimus, Articulus XXXV, Statutum 561.

[54] *Synodus Dioecesana Fargensis Secunda, 2-3 oct. 1951* (Milwauchiae: Ex Typographia Bruce, 1951), Pars Prima, Titulus Septimus, Articulus XXXV, Statutum 562.

THE DIOCESE OF FORT WAYNE–SOUTH BEND

(Established as the Diocese of Fort Wayne September 22, 1857; Redesignated the Diocese of Fort Wayne–South Bend on July 22, 1960.)

Synod of November 11, 1903:

Nulla unquam occasione licebit pecuniam ad foras ecclesiae exigere ut fideles ingredi et divinis mysteriis interesse possint, nisi ab adultis qui Missam audire cupiant quae specialis est puerorum.[55]

THE DIOCESE OF GALVESTON-HOUSTON

(Prefecture Apostolic erected at Galveston in 1838; Raised to the status of a Vicariate Apostolic in 1841; Created a diocese in 1847; Redesignated the Diocese of Galveston-Houston on July 25, 1959.)

VII Synod (April 23, 1930):

Entrance to the church for all services must be entirely gratuitous, all customs to the contrary notwithstanding.[56]

THE DIOCESE OF GRAND RAPIDS

(Established May 19, 1882.)

I Synod (September 18, 1903):

Pastor curabit ut singuli, qui ad suam ecclesiam pertinent saltem unam sedem conducant, ut ex hujusmodi reditibus et oblationibus inter Divina officia habendis, decenti pastoris et ecclesiae sustentationi sat provideatur. Vide tamen in appendice Decr. Conci. Plen. Balt. III n. n. 288 et 289, ubi damnatur praxis "pecuniam exigendi ad fores ecclesiae Dominicis ac Festis diebus, ut quis ingredi possit ac sacrosancto missae sacrificio interesse." [57]

55 *Synodus Dioecesana Wayne-Castrensis, 11 nov. 1903* (Nostrae Dominae, Indiana: Typis Universitatis [no date given]), Pars Secunda, Caput Sextum, Num. 101.

56 *Synodus Dioecesana Galvestoniensis Septima, 23 april. 1930* [no place or date of publication given], Section II, Title "Churches," Paragraph 11.

57 *Synodus Dioecesana Grandormensis Prima, 18 sept. 1903* [no place or

THE DIOCESE OF KANSAS CITY–ST. JOSEPH

(Diocese of Kansas City established September 10, 1880; Diocese of St. Joseph established March 3, 1868; Redesignated the Diocese of Kansas City–St. Joseph on August 29, 1956.)

II Synod (April 9, 1912):

> Omnes fideles ex propriis ecclesiam et scholam parochialem sustentare sub gravi se teneri sciant. Rectores modo paterno, sed efficaci, ad id praestandum eos inducant, semper exceptis pauperibus, qui quod tribuant non habent. Si ecclesia satis ampla inveniatur, sufficiens numerus scamnorum pro fidelibus procuretur; sin minus, ea pecuniae vel per familias vel per capita collectio adhibeatur quae nomine *subscriptions* audit. Scamna juxta prudens rectoris judicium ad tempus sive brevius sive longius locari possunt. Nulla unquam occasione licebit pecuniam ad foras ecclesiae exigere, ut fideles ingredi et divinis mysteriis interesse possint.[58]

III Synod (April 20, 1920):

The wording of the II Synod is repeated verbatim.[59]

IV Synod (October 30, 1928):

This Synod re-enacted the Statutes of the III Synod, with but a few corrections and additions. The statute pertaining to the matter in question remained in force, unchanged.[60]

---

date of publication given], Pars Secunda, Caput LVIII, Num. 331. Cf. also Appendix XV, "De Modis Pecunias Colligendi," in which Statutes No. 288 and 289 of the III Plenary Council of Baltimore are quoted verbatim.

58 *Decreta Synodi Dioecesanae Kansanopolitanae Secundae, 9 april. 1912* (Atchison, Kans.: Abbey Student Press, St. Benedict's College, 1912), Caput XVIII, Par. 1, Statutum 175.

59 *Statuta Dioecesana—Decreta Synodi Dioecesanae Kansanopolitanae Tertiae, 20 april. 1920* (Atchison, Kansas: Abbey Student Press [no date given]), Caput XVII, Par. 1, Statutum 197.

60 *Synodus Dioecesana Kansanopolitana Quarta, 30 oct. 1928* [no place or date of publication given].

THE DIOCESE OF LA CROSSE

(Erected in 1868.)

III Synod (April 27, 1955):

a. It is absolutely forbidden for all priests, whether diocesan or religious, to collect money at the entrance of the church or to have the ushers do so. However, receptacles in which parish envelopes can be deposited are permitted at the rear of the church.
b. Voluntary offerings only (i.e., plate collections) may be collected during divine services according to local custom.[61]

THE DIOCESE OF LAFAYETTE

(Established January 11, 1918.)

IV Synod (December 28, 1953):

Admission to the church for sacred rites must be entirely free, and every custom to the contrary is reprobated (Canon 1181).[62]

THE DIOCESE OF MANCHESTER

(Established in 1884.)

I Synod (November 4, 1886):

Penitus prohibemus ne in Dominicis ac Festis diebus, aut aliquo alio tempore in hac Nostra Dioecesi, quacumque de causa, a fidelibus exigatur, ut ad fores ecclesiae pecuniam solvant, aut chartulas pecunia emptas exhibeant antequam ipsis pateat ad sacrum aedificium ingressus. Con. III., No. 288; Con. II., No. 397.[63]

61 *Third Synod of the Diocese of La Crosse, April 27, 1955* (La Crosse, Wisc.: G. A. Keller Print [no date given]), Section VI, Article "A," Statute 388, par. a, b.

62 *Fourth Diocesan Synod of the Diocese of Lafayette, December 28, 1953* [no place or date of publication given], Book III, Part II, Title IX, No. 185.

63 *Constitutiones Dioecesanae ab . . . Dionysio Maria Bradley, Episcopo Manchesteriensi in Synodo Dioecesana Prima . . . Latae et Promulgatae,*

THE DIOCESE OF MOBILE-BIRMINGHAM

(*Established as a Prefecture Apostolic in 1824; Raised to the Vicariate Apostolic of Alabama in 1825; Became the Diocese of Mobile May 15, 1829; Redesignated the Diocese of Mobile-Birmingham July 9, 1954.*)

III Synod (June 24, 1921):

Quae in capite V, C. P. B. III, No. 288, "De Modis Prohibitis Pecunias Colligendi" sunt decreta, ab omnibus servari jubemus. Insuper nunquam licet sacerdoti aliquam partem oblati quod occasione Baptismi, Matrimonii, aut Funeris fideles solvant, suam facere, eo sub praetextu quod ratione doni personalis datur."[64]

THE DIOCESE OF MONTEREY-FRESNO

(*Erected December 3, 1922.*)

I Synod (October 29-30, 1929):

Nefas est pecuniam exigere ut quis possit ecclesiam ingredi ac sacrosancto Missae sacrificio interesse. Cf. C. B. 288.[65]

THE DIOCESE OF NASHVILLE

(*Established July 28, 1837.*)

I Synod (February 10, 1905):

The pastor will see that those who belong to his church rent at least one seat, and from these rents and the offertory collections a sufficient revenue be obtained for the proper

---

4 nov. 1886 (Manchester, N. H.: Typis Ormond D. Kimball, 1886), Titulus XIX, Num. 285.

[64] *Decreta Synodi Dioecesanae Mobiliensis Tertiae, 24 iun. 1921* (Mobile, Ala.: Ex Typographia Patterson Printing Co., Inc. [no date given]), Caput V, "De Variis Devotionis et Disciplinae Quaestionibus," Num. 77.

[65] *Statuta Dioecesis Montereyensis-Fresnensis . . . in Prima Synodo Dioecesana . . . Lata et Promulgata, 29-30 oct. 1929* (Fresni: Sumptibus Saint Columba Guild, Typis Crown Printing [no date given]), Titulus "De Cultu Divino," Statutum 23.

sustaining of the pastor and the Church. According to the decrees of the Second and Third Plenary Councils of Baltimore, the practice of "collecting money at the church doors on Sundays and Feast Days, in order that admission may be gained to hear Mass," is condemned.[66]

THE DIOCESE OF OKLAHOMA CITY AND TULSA

(Erected as a Vicariate Apostolic May 29, 1891; Became the Diocese of Oklahoma with the See at Oklahoma City August 17, 1905; Redesignated the Diocese of Oklahoma City and Tulsa November 14, 1930.)

I Synod (August 21, 1913):

Omnes fideles ex propriis ecclesiam et scholam parochialem sustentare sub gravi se teneri sciant. Rectores modo paterno, sed efficaci, ad id praestandum eos inducant, semper exceptis pauperibus, qui quod tribuant non habent. Si ecclesia satis ampla inveniatur, sufficiens numerus scamnorum pro fidelibus procuretur; sin minus ea pecuniae vel per familias vel per capita collectio adhibeatur quae nomine "subscriptions" audit. Scamna juxta prudens rectoris judicium ad tempus sive brevius sive longius locari possunt. Nulla unquam occasione licebit pecuniam ad foras ecclesiae exigere, ut fideles ingredi et divinis mysteriis interesse possint.[67]

THE DIOCESE OF PEORIA

(Established in 1877.)

III Synod (December 1, 1915):

Penitus prohibemus ne unquam in hac dioecesi quacumque de causa a fidelibus ad portas ecclesiae exigatur pecunia aut chartula pecunia empta; imo ne ulli omnino collectores ad ecclesiarum fores ponantur. (Conc. Plen. II, 397; III, 288, 289; Litt. Delegati Apost., 4, Nov. 1911).[68]

[66] *Synodus Dioecesana Nashvillensis Prima, 10 febr. 1905* [no place or date of publication given], Num. 179.

[67] *Statuta Dioeceseos Oklahomensis Quae in Synodo Prima . . . Sanxit et Promulgavit, 21 aug. 1913* (Ex Typis Orphanotrophii Sancti Josephi, Apud Oklahomam, in Oklahoma [no date given]), Titulus Sextus, Sectio 1, Num. 186.

[68] *Constitutiones Dioecesis Peoriensis Quae in Synodo Dioecesana Tertia*

THE DIOCESE OF PROVIDENCE

(*Established in 1872.*)

III Synod (December 21, 1887):

Praxis pecuniam exigendi ad fores ecclesiae, ut quis ingredi ac Sacrosancto Missae Sacrificio interesse possit, omnino damnata est et prorsus eliminanda.—Conc. Plen. Balt. III, 288.[69]

THE DIOCESE OF RALEIGH

(*Established as the Vicariate Apostolic of North Carolina March 3, 1868; Created the Diocese of Raleigh December 12, 1924.*)

I Synod (April 26, 1948):

There shall be no collection or offering as the people are entering the church.[70]

For a collection taken at the door as the people are leaving the church (in lieu of a second collection during Mass), taken up by Sisters or others, express permission must be obtained from the Ordinary.[71]

There shall be no compulsory collection or offering at any time before, during, or after divine services.[72]

There shall be no announcements of the sale of tickets outside the church doors after services.[73]

. . . *Latae et Promulgatae Fuerunt, 1 dec. 1915* (Bloomington, Illinois: Typis Pantagraph Printing and Stationery Co., 1915), Titulus XV, Num. 189.

69 *Acta et Decreta Synodi Dioecesanae Providentiensis Tertiae, 21 dec. 1887* ([no place of publication given]: Ex Typis Collegii Woodstockiensis, 1888), Caput XVI, Num. 147.

70 *First Synod of the Diocese of Raleigh, April 26, 1948* [no place or date of publication given], Statute 44.

71 *Ibid.*, Statute 45. (Statute 43 prescribes that there shall be no more than two collections taken up at the same Mass.)

72 *Ibid.*, Statute 46.

73 *Ibid.*, Statute 47.

THE DIOCESE OF SALT LAKE CITY

(Established as a Vicariate Apostolic November 23, 1886; Erected a Diocese January 27, 1891.)

I Synod (June 17, 1929):

Ingressus in ecclesiam ad sacros ritus omnino gratuitus remanere debet, nec licet quidquam ad januam exigere a fidelibus introire cupientibus.[74]

THE DIOCESE OF SCRANTON

(Established March 3, 1868.)

I Synod (May 4, 1949):

There shall be no collection or offering as the people are entering or leaving the church. (Cf. Canon 1181)[75]

THE DIOCESE OF SPRINGFIELD-IN-ILLINOIS

(Erected as the Diocese of Quincy July 29, 1853; See transferred to Alton January 9, 1857; Later transferred to Springfield October 26, 1923.)

II Synod (March 10, 1953):

Admission to the church for sacred functions must be absolutely free of charge; no money may be taken at the entrance of the church. We forbid any action or custom to the contrary.[76]

[74] *Statuta Dioecesis Lacus Salsi Lata ac Promulgata . . . in Synodo Dioecesana Prima, 17 iun. 1929* (Bronx, N. Y.: New York Catholic Protectory [no date given]), Caput X, Art. 2, Num. 203.

[75] *First Synod of the Diocese of Scranton, May 4, 1949* [no place or date of publication given], Title "The Sacraments," Statute 41, Paragraph 4.

[76] *Acta et Statuta Synodi Secundae Campifontis in Illinois, 10 mart. 1953* [no place or date of publication given], Part II, Chapter III, Article 1, Statute 114.

THE DIOCESE OF SYRACUSE

(Established November 20, 1886.)

I Synod (September 14, 1887):

> Monitis Conciliorum Plenariorum Baltimorensium II. et III. obsequentes, omnino prohibemus ne pecunia ad fores ecclesiae exigatur, ut ecclesiam intrare divinisque mysteriis adstare fidelis quivis possit. Imo stricte praecipimus ut in unaquaque ecclesia constituatur spatium liberum, ubi pretium sedis solvere aut non valentes aut nolentes, Sacro interesse et verbum Dei audire possint. (Conc. Plen. II. 397; III. 288, 289.)[77]

II Synod (September 30, 1890):

The legislation of the I Synod was re-enacted. This was supplemented with a few changes and additions.[78]

III Synod (November 6, 1893):

The legislation of the previous synods was re-enacted. A few changes and additions were incorporated.[79]

IV Synod (October 22, 1896):

The legislation of previous synods was re-enacted. Other changes and additions were made.[80]

V Synod (October 18, 1899):

The statutes of the previous synods were reconfirmed, and a few changes and additions were promulgated.[81]

[77] *Synodus Dioecesana Syracusana Prima, 14 sept. 1887* (Neo-Eboraci: Typis Societatis pro Libris Catholicis Evulgandis, 1887), Titulus XX, Num. 252.

[78] *Synodus Dioecesana Syracusana Secunda, 30 sept. 1890* (Syracusis, in Statu Neo-Eboracensi: Catholic Sun Press, 1890).

[79] *Synodus Dioecesana Syracusana Tertia, 6 nov. 1893* (Syracusis, in Statu Neo-Eboracensi, 1893).

[80] *Synodus Dioecesana Syracusana Quarta, 22 oct. 1896* (Syracusis, in Statu Neo-Eboracensi, 1896).

[81] *Synodus Dioecesana Syracusana Quinta, 18 oct. 1899* (Syracusis, in Statu Neo-Eboracensi, 1899).

VII Synod (October 17, 1905):

Reconfirmed all previous statutes. Added a few changes.[82]

VIII Synod (October 13, 1908):

Promulgated all previous statutes, together with a few changes and additions. [83]

XI Synod (September 8, 1921):

Repeated verbatim the wording of the I Synod.[84]

THE DIOCESE OF TOLEDO

(*Established April 15, 1910.*)

I Synod (November 4, 1941):

> It is strictly forbidden to ask or receive money at or near a church door either for entrance into the church or as an offering or payment for a seat in it. (Cf. Doc. Epis. 15.)[85]

Among the documents contained in an Appendix to this Synod is one entitled "Statement on church support by Bishop Schrembs." The following is an excerpt from that "Statement."

> By letter of October 29, 1911, the Apostolic Delegate called attention to the reprehensible practice of demanding money, and, by implication, its equivalent, at the doors of the church as a condition for entering the sacred edifice to assist at Mass and other religious services. His condemnation rests on the refusal, either direct or constructive, to admit people into the church unless they pay for a sitting. He ordered that such practice be eliminated entirely, and that bishops command all rectors of churches in their dioceses to discon-

[82] *Synodus Dioecesana Syracusana Septima, 17 oct. 1905* (Syracusis, in Statu Neo-Eboracensi: Catholic Sun Press, 1905).

[83] *Synodus Dioecesana Syracusana Octava, 13 oct. 1908* (Syracusis, in Statu Neo-Eboracensi: Catholic Sun Press, 1908).

[84] *Synodus Dioecesana Syracusensis Undecima, 8 sept. 1921* (Rochester, N. Y.: Typis Joannis P. Smith Printing Co., 1922), Titulus XX, Num. 254.

[85] *Acta et Decreta Synodi Dioecesanae Toletanae Primae, 4 nov. 1941* (Toleti: Cancellaria Curiae Dioecesanae, 1941), Pars Secunda, Caput V, Num. 380.

tinue the same, if it has been introduced, and not to permit it to be established, if it does not exist already. Every man, woman, and child, even the poorest, has a right to free admission to the church, and that privilege must be extended unstintingly. We therefore order pastors to see to it that no one, either councilmen or other officials, demand anything in money or tickets at the church door. It is, however, not at variance with any church regulation to solicit an offering for individual sittings from persons who have no pew and who wish to occupy one. In the case of such persons let the ushers show them to a pew in a gentlemanly way, and collect during the service the contribution, fixed by the pastor.

In conclusion we urge you to offer the poor every convenience in their attendance at divine service. Request them to call on you at the pastoral residence, and assign a seat in church to them. The poor ought to be so distributed in the church that their poverty will not be a cause of humiliation to them. Anything like the semblance of a Poor Man's Corner must not be tolerated in the House of God.[86]

THE DIOCESE OF TRENTON

(*Established July 15, 1881.*)

II Synod (June 25, 1896):

Monitis Conciliorum Plenariorum Baltimorensium II. et III. obsequentes, omnino prohibemus ne pecunia ad fores ecclesiae exigatur, ut ecclesiam intrare divinisque mysteriis adstare fidelis quivis possit. Imo stricte praecipimus ut in unaquaque ecclesia constituatur spatium liberum, ubi pretium sedis solvere aut non valentes aut nolentes, Sacro interesse et verbum Dei audire possint. (Conc. Plen. II. 397; III. 288, 289.)[87]

[86] *Ibid.*, Appendix Prima, Pars Secunda, "Documenta Episcopalia," Documentum 15.

[87] *Statuta Dioeceseos Trentonensis, Quae in Synodo Dioecesana Secunda . . . Sanxit et Promulgavit, 25 iun. 1896* (Trentonii: Typis "True American," 1897), Caput Septimum, Art. III, Num. 346.

THE DIOCESE OF WHEELING

(Established July 19, 1850.)

VII Synod (May 15, 1923):

Admission to divine service must be entirely free and every contrary custom is hereby reprobated (Can. 1181). We, therefore, order pastors to see to it that no one demands anything in money, or tickets previously sold, at the church door. The privilege of free admission to the house of God must be accorded, without discrimination, to every man, woman and child, even the poorest.[88]

THE DIOCESE OF WILMINGTON

(Established March 3, 1868.)

III Synod (November 17, 1898):

Ex Summi Pontificis Pii IX declaratione, utriusque Plenarii Concilii, tum Secundi, tum Tertii condemnatione, omnino abstinendum est a pecunia exigenda ad fores ecclesiarum ut fideles ingredi possint et divinis mysteriis adesse; quae praxis specimen vectigalis requisiti ut missae vel praedicationi quis adstare possit prae se ferre videtur. Spatium liberum et decens in unaquaeque ecclesia constituatur ubi fideles Sacro adesse et verbum Dei audire commode possint. (C. Plen. B. II. D. 397. C. Plen. B. III. D. 288, 289. Syn. Wilm. II. n. LII.)[89]

[88] *Statutes of the Diocese of Wheeling Promulgated at the* [*VII*] *Diocesan Synod held May 15, 1923* [no place or date of publication given], Part I, Chapter II, No. 65.

[89] *Statuta Dioeceseos Wilmingtoniensis Quae in Synodo Dioecesana Tertia . . . Sanxit et Promulgavit, 17 nov. 1898* (Baltimorae, Md.: Excudebant Foley Fratres, 1898), Caput Septimum, Articulus II, Num. 274.

CHAPTER VIII

THE APOSTOLIC DELEGATE'S SPECIFIC CONDEMNATION

In this country, on September 29, 1911, the "coup de grâce," so to speak, was dealt the practice of demanding money at the church door, when His Excellency The Most Reverend Diomede Falconio (later, Cardinal), Apostolic Delegate to the United States, elegantly and thoroughly condemned all such abuses in a Circular Letter addressed to the Bishops of America.[1]

His letter adds so much emphasis to all the previous repudiations, and is so exacting in its demand for immediate elimination of what, in fact, should have long since ceased, that it will be most fitting to quote it, in part, here:

> Your Lordship:
>
> On different occasions complaints have been made by various persons to this Delegation of the custom existing in some places as to the demand made at the doors of the church for money contributions to be given by those who are entering for the purpose of assisting at Mass or at other religious services.
>
> It was also said that in some localities tickets for entrance to the church for the same purpose were previously sold, and especially on the occasion of Christmas, Easter, etc., and were then demanded at the door of the church.
>
> The necessary investigation having been made, it was found to be only too true that these practices really exist in some of the parishes of the various dioceses, and I did not fail to call the attention of the Ordinaries to the matter.
>
> Since there is here a question of a practice really reprehensible and already condemned, a practice, moreover, which could easily spread, and thus give still greater scandal both to Catholics and to non-Catholics, I have deemed it my duty to make it the subject of a circular letter.
>
> It has long been known to all how strongly the Holy See

[1] As quoted in an article entitled "Collecting Money at Church Doors Unconditionally Abolished," *The Ecclesiastical Review,* XLV (1911), 594-596.

has reprobated all practices of this kind, their explicit condemnation having been made by Pius IX in the year 1862. Not less explicit are the provisions of the Second and Third Plenary Councils of Baltimore concerning this matter. . . . To these should be added the fact that the S. C. of the Propaganda addressed to all the Bishops of the United States a letter dated 15 August, 1869, which contained the following: [The Cardinal quotes here from the Admonition, as already treated in Chapter VI of this work.]

. . . I also wish to add that so recently as the 22nd of May, 1908, His Eminence, the Cardinal Prefect of the Propaganda, having received complaints concerning this matter, directed me to take measures to prevent the repetition of abuses of this kind, and I accordingly called the attention of the Bishop in whose diocese the abuse was verified to the matter.

After all that I have set forth, Your Lordship, to whom ecclesiastical decorum and the good of souls are above all other considerations, will, I am sure, be more than ever convinced of the necessity of completely eliminating all evils of this kind. I therefore request you to command all rectors of churches in your diocese to discontinue all these practices, if they have already been introduced, and by no means to permit them to be established, if they do not already exist.

I well know that in some churches money is collected at the door, not for mere entrance, but as a payment for a seat in the church. Even this practice cannot be tolerated, since it produces an undesirable impression on all, and has proved to be, in practice, the cause of many regrettable consequences.

This custom also is, moreover, directly and manifestly opposed to the spirit of the above-mentioned letter of the S. Congregation of the Propaganda, in which it is explicitly said, "*ne ulli omnino collectores . . . ad ecclesiarum fores ponantur.*" This custom, therefore, must also be abolished. In order, however, that the proper revenue from the pews be not lost, Your Lordship can devise some other method involving no objectionable features.

It need not be said that the present letter is not intended to prevent the distribution or taking up of tickets gratuitously given when special circumstances suggest their use.

I am sure that Your Lordship will put into execution without delay what I have here, as a matter of conscience, directed; instructing the clergy at the same time that if in the future further complaints concerning these matters are received and are found to be well grounded, the rector responsible for them will be condignly punished. . . .

This letter, together with all that has gone before, certainly sufficed to close the matter. The practice of demanding money from the faithful as they enter the church to be present for divine services, in whatever manner it may exist, stands many times condemned by the Church, must be done away with if it still exists in any place apart from where it is specifically allowed by the Holy See, and must never be permitted to exist in the future.

CHAPTER IX

THE PRACTICE IN OTHER COUNTRIES

ARTICLE 1. AUSTRALIA

It is interesting to note that the United States does not stand alone in being censured for collecting money from the faithful at the church door. A similar practice came to light on the occasion of a II Provincial Council in Australia, held in the city of Melbourne in the month of April, 1869. The Council was held under the auspices of The Most Reverend John-Bede Polding, O.S.B. (1794-1877), Archbishop of Sydney and Metropolitan of Australia (1842-1877).

The proceedings of the Council are recorded in the *Acta et Decreta Sacrorum Conciliorum Recentiorum.*[1] But, unfortunately, in the interest of brevity, only a portion of the Acts is recorded.[2]

When the original manuscript of transactions was sent to Rome, it contained a statement to the effect that on some particular occasion there was such a great crowd of people flocking from everywhere to attend a certain church that only those who presented tickets, which they had previously purchased, could be admitted.[3]

After studying the context, one could assume that the statement was intended, in fact, simply to assure the Holy See of the devotion of the people, and to establish a *bona fide* good impression as to their excellent attendance at certain Church functions.

As was the usual custom, when Cardinal Barnabo dispatched

[1] Cf. *Coll. Lac.*, III, 1059a-1088b.

[2] "Acta hujus Synodi maxima cura a R. P. Barsanti, O.S.F., concinnata sunt, quae tamen quum pro nostri operis ratione prolixiora sint, praecipua tantum excerpsimus."—*Ibid.*, III, 1059a.

[3] "Quamvis nullus ecclesiam ingredi posset nisi schedula munitus, pretioque soluto, attamen tantus erat populi concursus, ut ecclesia undequaque referta esset."—A quotation in a footnote, from the complete Acts of the Council; *ibid.*, III, 1084d, footnote 1.

the Sacred Congregation's official approval, he appended, July 16, 1872, a list of changes and corrections to be made.

It was prescribed, of course, that the practice of selling tickets for admittance to church should be done away with. Furthermore, the Sacred Congregation attached a transcript of the Admonition which had been sent to the Bishops of the United States, under the date of August 15, 1869,[4] and requested that copies of it be circulated among the Bishops of Australia.

So desirous was Cardinal Barnabo for expediting the process of doing away at once with what might lead to other abuses, that he personally drew up a revised copy of all those sections of the Acts and Decrees where the original wording regarding the practice was suppressed, changed, or supplanted.[5]

Thus it seems that the Sacred Congregation was taking no chances of having the custom prolonged or its condemnation misinterpreted. In forwarding to Australia the Admonition aimed at the United States, it seems that the Sacred Congregation—as a direct result of the Holy See's protracted dealings with the United States regarding the matter—meant to establish some sort of precedent which it could (and, *de facto,* did) use in dealing with such abuses as they turned up elsewhere.

Article 2. Concordats Specifically Allowing Money to be Demanded from the Faithful at the Church Door

As in all things which pertain strictly to ecclesiastical legislation, the Supreme Authority of the Church can and does make

[4] Cf. *supra,* Chapter VI, pp. 52-54.

[5] "Ac primo quidem super § *Quamvis* (pag. 12. actorum typis editorum, quae hisce literis adjiciuntur), ubi nimirum agitur de pretio soluto ad ingrediendam ecclesiam, praeter emendationem praescriptam ab EEm̃is Patribus atque in eo paragrapho calamo expressam, voluit S. Congregatio, ut per Ampl. Tuam communicetur Episcopis Australiae epistola S. hujus Congr. data die 15. Augusti 1869. ad Episcopos Americae Septentrionalis. Et quoniam de emendatione dixi, illud addam in genere, varias injunctas fuisse emendationes atque incisorum vel paragraphorum suppressiones tum in actis tum in decretis. Ut vero expeditius procederetur in exsequendis praedictis emendationibus, exemplar typis editum actorum ac decretorum tibi trado, in quo omnes ac singulae correctiones vel mutationes in textum introducendae indicantur, quas quidem Ampl. Tua executioni ad amussim mandandas curabit."—Cf. *Coll. Lac.,* III, 1084d-1085a.

exceptions in one form or another. From time to time the Holy See enters into Concordats with various sovereign powers.

> Concordats are solemn agreements between the Roman Pontiff and the civil ruler concerning matters of mutual interest to both high contracting parties. The object of these agreements is to avoid conflicts and disputes in matters falling within the twilight zone of both jurisdictions. The result often is a modification of the common law of the Church for the particular country in question. . . .[6]

Concerning the matter of taking up money at the door of the church, at least two Concordats entered into in recent years by the Holy See specifically allow such a practice. The very fact that the Supreme Pontiff sees fit to permit this custom to exist under certain circumstances demonstrates, therefore, that it is in no way contrary to the divine law.

On May 7, 1940, the Holy See concluded a Concordat with the Republic of Portugal. Article V of that Concordat allows money to be exacted at the church door. The Article reads thus:

> The Church can freely receive or exact from the faithful collections or any funds destined for the attainment of its own ends, particularly in the interior and at the doors of churches as well as of buildings and places which belong to her.[7]

On June 16, 1954, the Holy See entered into a Concordat with the Dominican Republic, and this agreement also provides that money may be collected at the church door. Article Twenty-three, Number four, of that Concordat states the following:

[6] Ramstein, *A Manual of Canon Law* (2 ed., Hoboken, N. J.: Terminal Printing & Publishing Co., 1948), p. 42.

[7] "La Chiesa può liberamente ricevere ed esigere dai fedeli collette e qualsiasi somma destinata all' attuazione dei suoi fini, segnatamente nell' interno e alla porta dei templi, nonchè degli edifici e luoghi ad essa appartenenti."—Cf. Concordato e Accordo Missionario con Il Portogallo—*AAS*, XXXII (1940), 221; *Raccolta di Concordati Su Materie Ecclesiastiche tra la Santa Sede e la Autorità Civili* (a cura di Angelo Mercati, 2 vols., Vol. I, nuova edizione anastatica con supplemento, Tipografia Poliglotta Vaticana, 1954), II, 234 (hereafter cited *Raccolta di Concordati*); Bouscaren, *The Canon Law Digest* (3 vols. with Supplements, Milwaukee: The Bruce Publishing Company, 1934-), II, 13.

> The Church can receive any donation destined for the fulfillment of its ends, and can exact offerings, especially inside or at the doors of churches and of the buildings and places that belong to her.[8]

Article 3. Particular Legislation

In an effort to obtain information relative to the matter at hand, the writer sent letters to twenty-eight of the principal episcopal sees outside the United States, with an inquiry whether or not particular legislation pertaining to door collections is in existence in those places.

Responses were received to almost all of the questionnaires, and the kindness of the Most Reverend Bishops and of the Very Reverend Chancellors in adding their comments and suggestions was of considerable assistance.

Of significant interest is the fact that in some European countries (notably in France) chairs may be rented at the rear of the church by those who desire such a convenience during divine services. In those countries the synodal statutes themselves make allowance for this legitimate custom of seat money, and quite often they prescribe the regulations to be followed in such a practice.

The only reference to an abuse contained in any of the letters was the mention of the fact that in some places collections or tickets had in the past been taken up at the church doors on the occasion of Midnight Mass on the Feast of Christmas. Wherever this practice was discovered, measures were instituted for its suppression.

Most of the archdioceses and dioceses from which responses were received have no particular laws relative to canon 1181. The following few statutes however indicate that the tone of the law abroad is almost the same as that in this country in so far as door collection prohibitions are concerned.

[8] "La Chiesa può ricevere qualsiasi donazione destinata all' attuazione dei suoi fini, e organizzare collette specialmente all' interno o alla porta dei templi e degli edifici e luoghi che le appartengano."—Cf. Concordato con La Repubblica Dominicana—*AAS,* XXXXVI (1954), 449; *Raccolta di Concordati,* II, 306-307.

The IV Plenary Council of Australia and New Zealand (September 4-12, 1937):

> Pariter vetatur sine Ordinarii licentia quominus pecunia colligatur ad fines pios a laices [*sic*] vel religiosis ad fores ecclesiae.[9]

The Plenary Council of Maynooth, Ireland (1927):

> Ingressus in ecclesiam ad sacros ritus sit omnino gratuitus, reprobata qualibet contraria consuetudine. Severe itaque prohibemus ne quis fidelium, Missam cupiens audire aliisve sacris functionibus adesse, ab ecclesia ideo repellatur quod nequeat aut nolit pecuniam solvere.[10]

The I Plenary Council of Quebec (1909):

> Omnino prohibetur ne taxa ad januas ecclesiarum exigatur uti conditio sine qua quis nequeat ingredi ad audiendam missam vel ad assistendum cuicumque alii functioni sacrae.[11]

The II Synod of the Diocese of Quebec (1940):

> Ingressus in ecclesiam ad sacros ritus sit omnino gratuitus, reprobata qualibet contraria consuetudine; et praesertim prohibetur ne taxa ad ianuas ecclesiae exigatur ut quis ingredi possit ad Missam audiendam vel ad assistendum cuicumque alii functioni sacrae.[12]

The Archdiocese of Rouen, France:

In 1806, Cardinal Cambacérès, Archbishop of Rouen, issued a decree concerning the assignment of places or seats in the church. The following is an excerpt from that decree:

[9] *Concilium Plenarium IV Australiae et Novae Zelandiae Habitum apud Sydney, A.D. 1937* (editio officialis, Manly: The Manly Daily, Pty. Ltd., 1939), Sectio III, Titulus X, Canon 521.

[10] *Concilium Plenarium Hiberniae, apud Maynutiam, 1927* [no place or date of publication given], Decretum 313.

[11] *Acta et Decreta Concilii Plenarii Quebecensis Primi, anno 1909* (Quebeci, 1912), Num. 635, a.

[12] *Acta et Decreta Synodi Dioecesanae Quebecensis Secundae anno 1940* (Quebeci, 1940), Decretum 309, § 1.

Churches are open freely to the public; hence it is expressly forbidden to collect anything within the churches and at their entrance, other than the price of the chairs, under any pretext whatsoever.[13]

The Synod of the Archdiocese of Rouen (1922):

Parish churches at which there is a resident pastor should be open all day. The same thing holds for mission churches, if responsible persons can be charged with opening and closing them. . . . Never is a ticket or an entrance fee to be demanded for admittance to any church. Sometimes, on the occasion of certain rare and unusual ceremonies, whose organization requires exceptional expenditures, the pastor is permitted to suspend, momentarily, the acquired right to occupy a personal place, and to subject this place to a higher rent. But even in this case some free places should be left in the church for the use of the first occupants.[14]

The Synod of the Archdiocese of Paris (1947):

Admission to the church is free (1181). Nevertheless an offering is asked of the faithful for the upkeep and the maintenance of the pews and furniture. Discretion should be used in the manner of taking up the collection, which should take place after the recitation or singing of the Creed.

In exceptional circumstances, when the pews have been reserved and some remuneration is allowed for special serv-

[13] "Les églises sont ouvertes gratuitement au public; en conséquence, il est expressément défendu de rien percevoir, dans les églises et à leur entrée, de plus que le prix des chaises, sous quelque prétexte que ce soit."—Cf. the "imperiale decretum" of Cardinal Cambacérès, Archbishop of Rouen, dated May 18, 1806, Titre I, Art. 1.

[14] "Les églises des paroisses où il y a un curé résidant doivent être ouvertes toute la journée. Il en est de même des églises desservies, si des personnes sûres peuvent se charger de les ouvrir et de les fermer. . . . Jamais une carte ni un droit d'entrée ne sont exigés pour pénétrer dans les églises. Toutefois, à l'occasion de certaines cérémonies rares et extraordinaires, dont l'organisation exige des dépenses exceptionnelles, il est permis au curé de suspendre momentanément le droit acquis à occuper une place personnelle et de soumettre cette place à une redevance plus élevée. Mais, même dans ce cas, des places gratuites doivent être laissées dans l'église à l'usage du premier occupant (C. 1181, C. 1266)."—*Statuts Synodaux du Diocese de Rouen, Anno 1922* [no place or date of publication given], Art. 301.

ices, a section of the church should always be provided where places are open and free of charge.[15]

15 "L'entrée des églises est gratuite (1181). Cependant une rétribution est demandée aux fidèles pour l'entretien et le remplacement des chaises et du mobilier. On usera de discrétion dans la manière de faire la quête, qui a lieu après la récitation ou le chant du Credo. Dans les circonstances exceptionnelles, où des chaises seraient réservées et comporteraient une rétribution pour des cérémonies spéciales, on maintiendra toujours une partie de l'église où les places seront libres et gratuites."—*Statuts Synodaux du diocèse de Paris, anno 1947* [no place or date of publication given], Titre IX, "Des Eglises," § 1, No. 192.

CONCLUSIONS

1. It is very probable that the practice of demanding money from the faithful at the door of the church originated in the United States, although it has not been entirely unknown in other countries.

2. The practice seems to have been initiated in good faith, as a means of obtaining additional revenue to help alleviate the rising temporal needs concomitant with the rapid growth, in the last century, of the Church in this country.

3. In some places this practice was in vogue as a method of obtaining contributions from those who had made no previous arrangements to pay the customary pew rent.

4. When the practice originally began, there was no intention of impeding the faithful in any way, physically or morally, from entering the church and being present for religious services. This argument, in fact, was later used as a defense on the part of some who continued the practice after it was initially forbidden.

5. The custom apparently proved relatively profitable; it undoubtedly spread rather rapidly; and additional abuses of one form or another began to creep in.

6. When successive prohibitions became more exacting, ways were discovered to circumvent the law, such as by collecting not at the door of the church itself, but from just inside the door, or in the vestibule.

7. In this country, apparent toleration of the abuse by some, together with ineffective enforcement of its condemnation by others, in spite of the Holy See's express desire to eliminate it immediately and entirely, led to its becoming so deeply entrenched in some areas that it came to be regarded as the customary procedure, not, however, without having induced a certain amount of scandal and grave embarrassment to many of the faithful, as well as having become the cause of much criticism directed toward the Church itself.

8. Whenever non-liturgical functions, such as concerts of sacred

music, literary or theological disputations, etc., are being held in church with the permission of the local ordinary, it is not in opposition to the law, apart from some *particular* prohibition, to request a moderate admission fee from those attending, provided that these functions have no direct connection with any sacred rite.

9. The sacred rites to which the faithful must be gratuitously admitted are the celebration of the Holy Sacrifice of the Mass, the recitation of the Divine Office, the administration of the Sacraments, and the conferral of the Sacramentals.

10. Wherever the above-mentioned sacred rites are performed, in a church, oratory, or elsewhere, no collections are to be taken up at the doors. Nor are there to be any baskets, tables, signs, tickets, or ushers to suggest, ask or request that a donation of any kind be made at the door, in the vestibule, at the entrances to the aisles, or in the aisles themselves. Moreover, the faithful must be freely admitted to the body of the church itself where the sacred functions which they wish to attend will take place.

11. A study of the history and development of the problem, in conjunction with all the special legislation affecting it, leads to this ultimate conclusion: The practice of demanding money from the faithful at the door of the church stands many times condemned. Apart from those places where the Holy See specifically allows it by way of a Concordat or otherwise, it must be universally abolished. Hence, no valid reason can be alleged for its existence anywhere today. Inasmuch as the abuse has been expressly reprobated, it may never be tolerated in any form in the future.

APPENDIX

PERTINENT PERIODICAL ARTICLES

(I)

The custom of collecting a specified fee at the church door from those who are not regular seat-holders, or who cannot be relied upon to comply in other ways with the demands to supply the parochial needs, has grown of late years. It is tolerated in spite of the prohibition of our Plenary Councils, and is sought to be justified on the ground that the people understand and approve this system as the easiest way of enforcing reasonable compliance with the divine law which obliges one to support religion in proportion to his ability and the needs of his parish. The requirements of public worship happen to be unusually stringent in a new country where the ministry of religion is an affair not of the State but of the individual, where churches, schools, parish houses, and manifold charitable institutions are to be supplied from the voluntary contributions of the faithful. This aspect of the work of upbuilding religion has won toleration in some places for what must have seemed to outsiders and to those not familiar with the motives of the Catholic hierarchy and clergy, an open violation of the laws of the Baltimore Council, which forbade the practice, "sicubi forte existat," because at that time the necessity of parish schools, of separate Catholic charity organization, and of proportionate expenditure for the maintenance of expensive church property, especially in large cities, was not so apparent or real as it is to-day.

But while criticism and condemnation, especially on the part of non-Catholics who understand neither the temper of the Catholic people nor the needs of Catholic worship, have largely exaggerated and misrepresented the practice of pastors seemingly exacting contributions at the church door from the people who felt the obligation of attending services therein, there has been unquestionably abuse on the part of the clergy in places where the needs of the parish did not warrant any such collecting, and where priests have apparently taken advantage of the generosity of the faithful to enrich themselves, to build needlessly costly residences for their own comfort, or to expend unnecessarily large sums for improvements dictated by personal vanity or notions of enterprise rather than by the needs of their flocks. This has caused comment and at times scandal.

Furthermore there is something utterly repugnant to the sense of propriety in the appearance of the money-changer at the gate of the temple or in the vestibule of the house of prayer. This appearance of scandal, even where there exists a proper motive for the act itself, is often injurious to the actual interests of religion. Hence, whatever excuse may be offered for the practice, whatever good may be furthered by the contributions thus enforced, the effect in another sense is hurtful to the community. As a matter of fact, priests are frequently stigmatized as "money grabbers," as vulgar browbeaters who exact a fee for attendance at sacred rites, where attendance is obligatory. The testaments of priests who now and then leave behind them sums disproportionate to their accredited incomes, for the use of their relatives or the contention of lawyers, or even for charities, give color to these insinuations of laggard Catholics and ignorant bigots.

Hence it is entirely just and wise to legislate against a practice that discredits religion, even if the said practice has some advantages in promoting the material upbuilding of the Catholic Church in America. Nor does it seem necessary to defend it as a necessity in the past. Where a pastor and his assistants devote themselves to the upbuilding of the spiritual Church by intelligent zeal and personal sacrifice, there will never be any real lack of the material things, especially such as would be supplied by morally enforced contributions at the door of the church. Most people love truth; but one must demonstrate it to them, not merely talk it at them. Love of truth begets charity, and charity grows with every stirring of generous impulse created by the words of a priest. To say that there are people who are hard-hearted and indifferent is a platitude. There are of course; but they are not made dutiful by browbeating them. A whole-souled priest is expected to change them by preaching and good example. To question the efficacy of the priestly life or of the teaching of the Gospel is to deny the eternal truth which we profess to inculcate by word and example.

The following Circular Letter of the Apostolic Delegate is therefore both reasonable in its demands on our obedience and helpful to edification. At the same time it is a very positive command which can be ignored only at the risk of violating priestly loyalty and obedience. (Following was the letter of the Most Reverend Diomede Falconio, dated September 29, 1911, previously discussed in Chapter VIII).[1]

(II)

"Fight fire with fire," is an old saying. It means in church economics: be mean with the mean, only be a little meaner. It has led many a pastor to use means and methods which he loathes, but which he felt constrained to employ in his struggles to induce his people to support their parish. It has tempted him to take up collections, hold illicit entertainments, scold and threaten, drive people out of the church, and make religion generally odious.

The vacation season has just closed. In the cities we are receiving all sorts of comments from our people. Most of these comments bear upon collections and especially upon being "held up" at churchdoors in summer resorts. Propriety and good taste apart, we all know that it is forbidden to charge a fee for admission to our churches. Legislation on that point is clear. But, like much more wise legislation, it is ignored, defeated, or openly violated. Nothing can be more scandalous than the table at the door, the efficient cashier (who is not infrequently the pastor or his assistant), and the sign announcing, "Seats 25 cents," or even the shameful, "Admission 25 cents."

There is no denying that many people are mean; that they will not give a cent to the church, if they can help it; that the parish needs money; that the church has been built large enough to accommodate the summer people; that there are extra services and therefore extra expenses on their account. The fact remains: it is wrong to hold up people who are going to Mass; it gives scandal to decent Catholics; it makes the priest who does it mean, abusive and hateful.

Of course, the above-mentioned abuse is not confined to the country. It is not uncommon in the largest cities. Some pastors justify themselves by providing a few free seats—a sort of "poverty corner." Others make the "dead line" a few feet beyond the entrance. Others, again, offer what they call free tickets to those who will call on them and explain their inability to pay.

As an alternative, many places have two collections. The first, at the Offertory, is for pew rent. The second, after the Communion, is for the voluntary offering. This method is less objectionable. But it has this grave defect. It en-

[1] Anon., "Collecting Money at Church Doors Unconditionally Abolished."—*The Ecclesiastical Review,* XLV (1911), 592-596.

tails money-changing during the divine service, or, where no change is given, it causes distraction by the march of the collectors, the passing of the plate, and, worst of all, the clink of the coins during the solemn part of the Mass. Further than this, it makes collecting a continuous performance. The collecting begins at the *Credo* and, with almost no interruption, continues until the very end of Mass. In fact, in some places, the celebrant has orders to interrupt the service and wait for the collectors to finish their work! When he finally receives the "all clear" signal, he may say the final prayers or give the last blessing.

At almost every clerical retreat, there is a conference on money-gathering. It is interesting to recall the comments which follow this conference. Most retreat masters are members of some religious Order. That, of course, condemns them forthwith.

"What does *he* know about it? It is easy for these guys to talk; I notice they want their pound of flesh when they give a mission or render a service; if you do not hand out the 'dough' to them, they blacklist you and leave you in the lurch."

"We know our people; the decent ones never complain; they understand; it is the 'pikers' that squeal; we are not running our churches to please Protestants."

"What does he want us to do? Live on air? Eat snowballs? Where is the interest coming from? If I don't pay my bills, the bishop will send some other priest who can and will pay them."

"These religious are not practical. It is all very well to quote Scaramelli. He is dead. He never ran a parish. These fellows don't understand our people and our problems."

Remarks like these are familiar to all priests. They lead to much discussion. They certainly provoke thought and prod the conscience. Sometimes they induce the younger or the more conscientious to inquire how they can avoid the abuse without curtailing their revenue. Often they consult the older and more successful pastors. Unfortunately, all the older men are not good advisers. The most successful men are not always the most priestly. Their advice may be deadly poison. Some of them do not hesitate to ridicule the criticism of the retreat master. They are like the advisers of the young King of Israel. They urge severity and more severity. Their experience and their prominence give weight to their advice. They often spoil a good purpose and oppose the work of the Holy Ghost. They send that young man home a confirmed "gold-digger," when honesty and truth would have saved him from that shameful—not to say wicked—method or practice.

Apart from the unlawfulness of door collections, it is bad business to have them. Everyone knows that contentment is invaluable. In fact, contentment is only another name for peace. When people feel that their church is run on a business basis, like a theatre or a pay-as-you-enter car, they cannot go to it or use it with anything like the spirit of love and devotion which should prevail. God does not want His house to be commercialized. While He does make it a duty to contribute to the work of religion, constraint is no part of His plan or policy. God wants *voluntary* service and *voluntary* contributions. His blessing does not and will not rest on the parish where money is squeezed out of the people. It will not do to name priests who have followed this method and who have been rewarded with what the world calls "success." We are not dealing with worldly standards. We are trying to look at this matter in the light of the sacerdotal ideal. Does anyone dare entertain the thought that Christ our Lord would charge men an admission fee to hear Him or to participate in His sacraments or His holy sacrifice? Can anyone picture Him standing at the door of a church, watching those who enter and noting what they hand to the money changers? Can anyone conceive Him, calling out with a vulgarity which humor cannot excuse: "Have your money ready! Get your dime or your quarter ready!"

We believe that God's blessing is essential to success. "Without Me," said our Lord to His disciples, "you cannot do *anything*." "Unless the Lord build the house, in vain do they labor who (seek to) build it."

Appearances are deceptive. Magnificent churches are not always noble monuments. If they have been built with pride or extortion, they do not glorify God or show forth the virtue of the builders. Does it not happen that many a splendid church has been the occasion of a quarrel between the pastor and parishioners, which ended in estrangement or even in the loss of faith for a whole family?

No, for God's sake, *"auferte ista hinc!"* Take these things hence! Take down the signs! Remove the tables! Tear up the tickets! The House of God is a sacred place. If we treat it with reverence and show our people that we love it and believe in what it represents, we shall soon find them willing and even anxious to do their part for the church and the school and for us. There will always be shirkers. We can convert some—not all. But let us learn from the Lord how to treat them. "Wait," He said, "for the harvest!" Do not ruin the wheat by pulling up the cockle.

If you find it necessary, have two collections, but try the plan of having one. Tell the people why you do it. Show them that you are consulting the decency of divine worship, and that you are treating them as intelligent conscientious co-workers with the Lord. Several parishes have tried this method with complete satisfaction. None of them would go back to the old method, even if it would be more profitable. Some find that they receive less in one collection, but they are satisfied to wait. It takes years to teach some lessons. At least, they are not ashamed of their method, and they know they have the respect and appreciation of the people.

Some day we shall see the futility of these old methods. Some genius, or the collective genius of the clergy, will devise a plan of church support which will do away with the uncertainty of haphazard, give-what-you-like collections. Even now some have found relief in the budget system and the weekly envelope. In some places, the pastor asks the wage-earners to agree to give so much a year to the church. He does away with fairs, bazaars, and all entertainments. He has no special collections, except for *diocesan* purposes. He never "talks money" except once a year, when he explains the plan. He has only one collection on Sunday. In that he asks for twenty-five cents at least. The subscription can be paid at once, twice a year, four times a year, or once a month. Most people find it convenient to give a certain sum each month. On the second Sunday a printed list is given out. It contains the names of the subscribers and the sums given, except in cases where the donor requests that his name be not printed.

In one parish, this plan has been in effect for twelve years. There are 6,000 souls. They give about $18,000 a year. This supplements the church revenue so well that the parish is out of debt. In fact, it has a very substantial fund invested, the income of which is more than sufficient to pay the cost of maintaining the school.

The people like the plan, and are proud to tell their friends: "*Our* priests do not talk money or take up collections."[2]

[2] Rt. Rev. Msgr. John L. Belford, D.D., "Church Door Collections."—*The Homiletic and Pastoral Review* (*Homiletic Monthly and Catechist*, Vols. I-XVII, New York, 1901-1917; *The Homiletic Monthly*, Vol. XVIII, New York, 1918; *The Homiletic Monthly and Pastoral Review*, Vols. XIX, XX, New York, 1918-1920; *The Homiletic and Pastoral Review*, Vol. XXI- , New York, Oct. 1920-), XXVIII (Oct. 1927-March 1928), 138-142

(III)

Question: Will you kindly solve for me the following question? A member of my parish takes the seat money at the church door on Sundays. During the winter months I find it necessary to close the inside doors of the vestibule, the man in question remaining outside of them. In this way he is prevented from being present inside the church during much of Mass time. When this occurs, is his obligation to hear Mass satisfied? It would seem a hardship to ask him to attend another Mass in view of the service that he renders. On the other hand he is deprived of the spiritual advantage of undisturbed attention at the Holy Sacrifice.

Response: "Undisturbed attention," and "the presence inside the church" proper, are not required to fulfill the obligation of hearing Mass. The church and the theologians are very lenient in their interpretation of the requirements. Whether the person in question *de facto* can sufficiently attend, depends on the vestibule doors of the particular church. Conceivably, *in abstracto,* he can be regarded as in a situation that permits of his fulfilling the precept.

The rub, however, is not on the points of presence and attention. For, *in concreto,* granting that his situation is favorable, how can this be squared with the "unqualified prohibition of collectors at church doors"? He is outlawed, and therefore his occupation during Mass can hardly be considered as an "accessio sacrificii." It does not appear that the premises of lenient interpretation as to the fulfillment of the Mass obligation should be put upon this condemned practice.[3]

[3] Anon., "Collections at Church Door."—*The Ecclesiastical Review,* LXXIX (1928), 647.

BIBLIOGRAPHY

SOURCES

Acta Apostolicae Sedis, Commentarium Officiale, Romae, 1909-1929; Civitate Vaticana, 1929-

Acta et Decreta Concilii Plenarii Baltimorensis Tertii, A.D. MDCCCLXXXIV, Baltimorae: Typis Joannis Murphy et Sociorum, 1886.

Acta et Decreta Concilii Plenarii Quebecensis Prima, anno 1909, Quebeci, 1912.

Acta et Decreta Conc. Provincialis Ultraiectensis, anno 1934, Institutum Surdo-mutorum in Gestel S. Michaelis [no date given].

Acta et Decreta Sacrorum Conciliorum Recentiorum, Collectio Lacensis, 7 vols., Friburgi Brisgoviae, 1870-1892.

Acta et Decreta Synodi Dioecesanae Quebecensis Secundae, anno 1940, Quebeci, 1940.

Acta et Decreta Synodi Provincialis Ruthenorum Galiciae, Habitae Leopoli An. 1891, Romae: Ex Typographia Polyglotta S. C. De Propaganda Fide, 1896.

Acta et Decreta Tertii Concilii Provincialis Westmonasteriensis, 13-24 iul. 1859, Londini: Typis Tomae Jones, 1854 [*sic*].

Bullarum Diplomatum et Privilegiorum Romanorum Pontificum Taurinensis Editio, 24 vols. and Appendix, Augustae Taurinorum, 1857-1872.

Canon Law Digest, The, edited by T. Lincoln Bouscaren, 4 vols. with Supplements, Milwaukee: The Bruce Publishing Co., 1934- .

Codex Iuris Canonici Pii X Maximi iussu digestus Benedicti Papae XV auctoritate promulgatus, Romae: Typis Polyglottis Vaticanis, 1917.

Codicis Iuris Canonici Fontes, cura Emi Petri Card. Gasparri editi, 9 vols. (Vols. VII-IX ed. cura et studio Emi Iustiniani Card. Serédi), Romae [postea civitate Vaticana]: Typis Polyglottis Vaticanis, 1923-1939.

Collectanea S. Congregationis de Propaganda Fide, 2 vols., Romae: Typographia Polyglotta S. C. de Propaganda Fide, 1907.

Concilii Plenarii Baltimorensis II., in Ecclesia Metropolitana Baltimorensi, a die VII. ad diem XXI. Octobris, A.D. MDCCCLXVI., Habiti, et a Sede Apostolica Recogniti, Acta et Decreta, Baltimorae: Excudebat Joannes Murphy, 1868.

Concilium Plenarium Hiberniae, apud Maynutiam, anno 1927 [no place or date of publication given].

Concilium Plenarium IV Australiae et Novae Zelandiae Habitum apud Sydney, A.D. 1937, editio officialis, Manly: The Manly Daily, Pty. Ltd., 1939.

Corpus Iuris Canonici, 2 ed., Lipsiensis, post Aemilii Ludovici Richteri curas instruxit Aemilius Friedberg, 2. vols., Lipsiae, 1879-1881. Editio anastatice repetita, 1922.

Decreta Synodi Plenariae Episcoporum Hiberniae Apud Thurles Habitae, Anno MDCCCL, Dublinii: Apud Jacobum Duffy, 1851.

Decreta Tertiae Synodi Dioecesanae Westmonasteriensis, 10 febr. 1858, Londini: Typis Richardson et Filii, 1858.

Decreta Quartae Synodi Dioecesanae Westmonasteriensis, 18 nov. 1862, Londini, 1863.

Decreta Quintae Synodi Dioecesanae Westmonasteriensis, 14 dec. 1865, Londini, 1865.

Juris Pontificii de Propaganda Fide Pars Prima, Complectens Decreta Instructiones Encyclicas Litteras Etc. ab Eadem Congregatione Lata, cura ac studio Raphaelis de Martinis, 7 vols. in 8, Romae: Ex Typographia Polyglotta S. C. de Propaganda Fide, 1888-1897; *Pars Secunda,* 1 vol., Romae, 1909.

New Testament of Our Lord and Savior Jesus Christ, The, Confraternity of Christian Doctrine edition, Paterson, N. J.: St. Anthony Guild Press, 1941.

Quarta Synodus Dioecesana Birminghamiensis, 9 iun. 1869, Derbiae: Ex Typis Richardson et Filii, 1869.

Raccolta di Concordati su Materie Ecclesiastiche tra la Santa Sede e le Autorità Civili, a cura di Angelo Mercati (2 vols., Vol. I, nuova edizione anastatica con supplemento), Tipografia Poliglotta Vaticana, 1954.

Rules and Directions for the Administration of the Temporal Affairs of the Church in the Diocese of Cleveland, Cleveland: Fairbanks, Benedict & Co., Printers, 1863.

Rules and Directions for the Administration of the Temporal Affairs of the Church in the Diocese of Cleveland [Issued July 28, 1857], Cleveland: Henry Kramer, 1857.

Rules and Directions for the Administration of the Temporal Affairs of the Church in the Diocese of Detroit, Detroit: John Slater, 1862.

Schroeder, H. J., *Canons and Decrees of the Council of Trent, Original Text with English Translation,* St. Louis: B. Herder Book Co., 1950.

Sexta Synodus Dioecesana Westmonasteriensis, 13 iun. 1866, Londini, 1866.

Sínodo Diocesano de Madrid-Alcalá, anno 1948 [no place or date of publication given].

Statuts Synodaux du Diocèse de Paris, anno 1947 [no place or date of publication given].

Statuts Synodaux du Diocese de Rouen, anno 1922 [no place or date of publication given].

Synode de Montréal, Le, 9 décembre 1953, Archevêché de Montréal, 1953.

Synodus Provincialis Ruthenorum, Habita in Civitate Zamosciae Anno MDCCXX, Romae: Ex Typographia Polyglotta S. C. De Propaganda Fide [no date given].

PROVINCIAL COUNCILS

(The United States of America)

THE PROVINCE OF BALTIMORE

Concilia Privincialia, Baltimori habita ab anno 1829, usque ad annum 1840 [I, oct. 1829; II, oct. 1833; III, oct. 1837; IV, maii. 1840], Baltimori: Apud Joannem Murphy, 1842.

Concilium Baltimorense, Provinciale Secundum, 20-27 oct. 1833, Baltimori: Ex Typis J. D. Toy [no date given].

Concilium Baltimorense Provinciale VIII, 6-13 maii. 1855, Baltimori: Apud Joannem Murphy et Socios, 1857.

Concilium Baltimorense Provinciale IX, 2-9 maii. 1858, Baltimori: Apud Joannem Murphy et Socios [no date given].

Concilii Provincialis Baltimorensis X . . . Acta et Decreta, 25 april.–2 maii. 1869, Baltimorae: Typis Joannis Murphy, 1870.

THE PROVINCE OF CINCINNATI

Concilium Cincinnatense Provinciale I, 13-20 maii. 1855, Cincinnati: John P. Walsh, Printer and Publisher [no date given].

Concilium Cincinnatense Provinciale II, 2-9 maii. 1858, Cincinnati: John P. Walsh, Printer and Publisher [no date given].

Concilium Cincinnatense Provinciale III, 28 april.–5 maii. 1861, Cincinnati: Sumptibus Fratrum Benziger [no date given].

Acta et Decreta Quatuor Conciliorum Provincialium Cincinnatensium 1855-1882, Cincinnati: Typis Benziger Fratrum, 1886.

Concilium Cincinnatense Provinciale V, 19-26 maii. 1889, Cincinnati, O.: Keating & Co., 1893.

THE PROVINCE OF MILWAUKEE

Acta et Decreta Concilii Provincialis Milwaukiensis Primi, 23-30 maii. 1886, Milwaukiae: Hoffman Fratres Typographi Summi Pontificis, 1888.

THE PROVINCE OF NEW ORLEANS

Concilium Provinciale Primum Provinciae Neo-Aurelianensis, 20-27 ian. 1856 [no place or date of publication given].

Concilium Neo-Aurelianense Provinciale Secundum, 22-29 ian. 1860, Neo-Aureliae: Ex Typis Propagatoris Catholici, 1864.

Concilium Neo-Aurelianense Provinciale Tertium, 8-19 ian. 1873, Neo-Aureliae: Ex Typis Propagatoris Catholici, 1875.

THE PROVINCE OF NEW YORK

Concilium Neo-Eboracense Primum, 1-8 oct. 1854, Neo-Eboraci: Apud Eduardum Dunigan et Fratrem, 1855.

Concilium Provinciale Neo-Eboracense III, mense iunii, anno MDCCCLXI Celebratum, Neo-Eboraci: Apud Eduardum Dunigan et Fratrem, 1862.

Acta et Decreta Concilii Provincialis Neo-Eboracensis IV, 23-30 sept. 1883, Neo-Eboraci: Typis Societatis Pro Libris Catholicis Evulgandis, 1886.

THE PROVINCE OF PHILADELPHIA

Decreta Concilii Provincialis Philadelphiensis I, mense maii, anno 1880, Philadelphia, Pa.: Catholic Standard and Times Print [no date given].

THE PROVINCE OF PORTLAND IN OREGON

Acta et Decreta Conciliorum Provinciae Oregonopolitanae Annis [I: 28, 29 febr.-1 mart.] 1848 [II: 16-18 aug.] 1881 et [III: 18-21 oct.] 1891 Celebratorum, Mount Angel, Ore.: Typis Monasterii S. Benedicti, 1895.

Acta et Decreta Concilii Provincialis Portlandensis in Oregon Quarti, 8-10 sept. 1932, Portland, Oregon: Sentinel Printery, 1934.

THE PROVINCE OF ST. LOUIS

Acta et Decreta Concilii Provincialis Primi, mensi octobri, A.D. 1855, Sancti Ludovici Habiti, S. Ludovici: Apud Georgium Knapp & Co., 1858.

Concilium Provinciale Secundum . . . Sancti Ludovici Habitum, mense sept., anno 1858, S. Ludovici: Apud Georgium Knapp & Co., 1859.

THE PROVINCE OF SAN FRANCISCO

Concilii Provincialis S. Francisci I . . . Acta et Decreta, 26 april.-3 maii. 1874, Sancti Francisci: Ex Typographia Thomas et Soc., 1875.

Concilii Provincialis S. Francisci II . . . Acta et Decreta, 30 april.-4 maii. 1882, Sancti Francisci: Ex Typographia P. J. Thomas, 1883.

ARCHDIOCESAN SYNODS

(The United States of America)

THE ARCHDIOCESE OF BALTIMORE

Statuta Synodi Baltimorensis I, 7-10 nov. anno 1791 Celebratae, as found in *Concilia Provincialia, Baltimori habita ab anno 1829, usque ad annum 1840,* Baltimori: Apud Joannem Murphy, Typographum ac Bibliopolam, 1842.

Synodus Dioecesana Baltimorensis II, 8-10 nov. 1831, Baltimori: Ex Typis J. D. Toy, 1831.

Synodus Dioecesana Baltimorensis, mense iunio 1853 Habita, Baltimori: Ex Typis Joannis Murphy et Sociorum, 1853.

Synodus Dioecesana Baltimorensis, mense iunio 1857 Habita, Baltimori: Apud Joannem Murphy et Socios, 1857.

Synodus Dioecesana Baltimorensis, mense maii. 1863 Habita, Baltimore: Apud Joannem Murphy et Socios, 1863.

Acta Synodi Dioecesanae Baltimorensis Sextae, 24 maii. 1865, Baltimori: Typis Kelly et Piet, 1865.

Synodus Dioecesana Baltimorensis Septima, 3 sept. 1868, Baltimorae: Excudebat Joannes Murphy, 1868.

Synodus Dioecesana Baltimorensis Octava, 27 aug. 1875, Baltimorae: Excudebant Joannes Murphy et Socii, 1876.

Synodus Dioecesana Baltimorensis Nona, 24 sept. 1886, Baltimorae: Excudebant Foley Fratres, 1886.

THE ARCHDIOCESE OF BOSTON

Synodus Dioecesana, Bostoniensis I, 21 aug. 1842, Bostoniae: Ex Typis Patritii Donahoe [no date given].

Constitutiones Dioecesanae . . . in Synodo Dioecesana Secunda . . . Latae et Promulgatae, 5 nov. 1868 [no place or date of publication given].

Constitutiones Dioecesanae . . . Latae et Promulgatae, anno 1886, Bostoniae, 1886.

Constitutiones Dioeceseos Bostoniensis quae in Synodo Dioecesana Quinta . . . Latae et Promulgatae Fuerunt, 11 feb. 1909, Bostoniae, Mass.: Ex Typis "Washington Press," 1910.

Constitutiones Dioeceseos Bostoniensis quae in Synodo Dioecesana Sexta . . . Latae et Promulgatae Fuerunt, 7 april. 1919, Bostoniae: Ex Typis "Washington Press," 1919.

Acta et Statuta Synodi Bostoniensis Septimae, 29 maii. 1952 [no place or date of publication given].

THE ARCHDIOCESE OF CHICAGO

Synodus Dioecesana Chicagensis [sic] *mense augusti 1860 Habita,* Chicagiae: Apud Tobey Fratres Typographos, 1860.

Synodus Dioecesana Chicagiensis Prima [sic], *13 dec. 1887,* Chicagiae: Ex Typis Cameron, Amberg et Sociorum, 1887.

Synodus Dioecesana Chicagiensis Secunda, 3 iun. 1902, Chicagiae: Ex Typis Cameron, Amberg, et Sociorum, 1902.

Synodus Dioecesana Chicagiensis . . . Tertia, 14 dec. 1905, Chicagine: Typis Mandarunt Cameron, Amberg Sociique, 1906.

THE ARCHDIOCESE OF CINCINNATI

Statuta Dioecesana ab . . . Joanne Baptista Purcell, Archiepiscopo Cincinnatensi . . . in variis synodis . . . Celebratae sunt, Lata et Promulgata, Cincinnati: John P. Walsh, 1865.

Synodus Dioecesana Cincinnatensis Secunda, 19-21 oct. 1886 [no place or date of publication given].

Synodus Dioecesana Cincinnatensis Tertia, 9 nov. 1898 [no place or date of publication given].

Fifth Synod of the Archdiocese of Cincinnati, December 14, 1954 [no place or date of publication given].

THE ARCHDIOCESE OF DENVER

Synodus Dioecesana Denveriensis Prima, 2 aug. 1889, Las Vegas: Ex Typis Societatis Jesu, 1889.

Synodus Dioecesana Denverensis [sic] *Secunda, 31 iul. 1891,* Las Vegas: Ex Typis Societatis Jesu, 1891.

Synodus Dioecesana Denverensis [sic] *I, II, III, 2 aug. 1889, 31 iul. 1891, 4 aug. 1893,* Las Vegas: Ex Typis Societatis Jesu, 1894.

Synodus Dioecesana Denveriensis Quarta, 15 iul. 1904, Las Vegas: Ex Typis Societatis Jesu, 1905.

THE ARCHDIOCESE OF DETROIT

Constitutiones Synodi Dioecesanae Detroitensis Primae, 8-12 oct. 1859, Detroiti: Ex Typis Joannis Slater, 1859.

Synodus Dioecesana Detroitensis Secunda, 28-30 sept. 1862, Detroiti: Ex Typis Joannis Slater, 1862.

Acta et Constitutiones Synodi Dioecesanae Detroitensis Quartae, 15-18 oct. 1878, Detroiti: Free Press Book and Job Printing House, 1878.

Acta et Constitutiones Synodi Dioecesanae Detroitensis Quintae, 16, 18, 19 iul. 1881, Detroiti: Typis M'Cormack & Co., 1881.

Acta et Constitutiones Synodi Dioecesanae Detroitensis Sextae, 20, 21 iul. 1885, Detroiti: Typis Kilroy et Brennan, 1881 [*sic*].

Synodus Dioecesana Detroitensis Septima, 19 aug. 1886, Marshall, Mich.: Marshall Publishing Company, 1886.

Synodus Detroitensis Octava, 19 dec. 1944 [no place of publication given]: Michigan Catholic Press, 1950.

THE ARCHDIOCESE OF DUBUQUE

Statuta Lata et Promulgata ab . . . Episcopo Dubuquensi, in Synodo Prima Dioecesana, 3 maii. 1860, Dubuquii: Ex Typis Rich & Ryan, 1871.

Synodus Dioecesana Dubuquensis Tertia, 2 april. 1905 [no place or date of publication given].

Synodus Dioecesana Dubuquensis Quarta, 31 mart. 1908 [no place or date of publication given].

Synodus Dioecesana Dubuquensis Quinta, 16 nov. 1911 [no place or date of publication given].

Statutes of the Archdiocese of Dubuque Enacted and Promulgated . . . in the Eighth Archdiocesan Synod, December 10, 1947 [no place or date of publication given].

THE ARCHDIOCESE OF HARTFORD

Decreta Synodi Hartfordiensis Primae, 16-22 oct. 1854, Providentiae: Ex Typis Benjamin T. Albro, 1855.

Constitutiones Synodi Hartfordiensis II, 12 sept. 1878, Hartford, Conn.: Ex Typis "The Case, Lockwood, et Brainard Company," 1878.

Constitutiones Synodi Hartfordiensis IV [*sic*, erroneously titled IV instead of III], *10 aug. 1886*, Hartford, Conn.: Ex Typis "The Case, Lockwood et Brainard Company," 1887.

Decreta Synodorum Hartfordiensium in unum volumen Collecta, Hartfordiae, Conn.: Ex Typis Ephem. Dioec. vulgo "The Catholic Transcript," 1902.

THE ARCHDIOCESE OF INDIANAPOLIS

Acta et Decreta Quinque Synodorum Dioeceseos Vincennopolitanae [I: 5-7 maii. 1844; II: 10-12 dec. 1878; III: 30 nov.–2 dec. 1880; IV: 30 nov.–1 dec. 1886; V: 29-30 april. 1891], Indianapoli: Typis Carlon & Hollenbeck, 1891.

Statuta Dioecesis Indianapolitanae Lata ac Promulgata . . . in Synodo Dioecesana Sexta, 20 maii. 1937, Indianapolis, Indiana: Typis Harrington & Folger, Inc., 1937.

Statuta Archidioeceseos Indianapolitanae Lata ac Promulgata . . . in Synodo Archidioecesana [sic] (*I*) *Septima, 21 maii. 1947*, Indianapolis, Indiana: Standard Printing Company, 1947.

THE ARCHDIOCESE OF KANSAS CITY IN KANSAS

Statuta ab . . . Episcopo Leavenworthiensi in Synodo Dioecesana Prima . . . Lata et Promulgata, 17-19 oct. 1880, Leavenworth, Kan.: Ex Typis Ketcheson, 1881.

Synodus Dioecesana Leavenworthensis [sic] *Secunda, 10, 11 aug. 1887*, Laurentii, Kan.: Ex Typis P. T. Foley, 1887.

Decreta Synodi Dioecesanae Leavenworthiensis Secundae . . . cum aliquot Mutationibus et Emendationibus, 8 dec. 1907, Atchinson [*sic*], Kansas: Abbey Student Press [no date given].

Statuta Dioecesana—Decreta Synodi Dioecesanae Leavenworthensis [sic] *Tertiae, 6 iun. 1922* [no place or date of publication given].

Statuta Synodi Kansanopolitanae in Kansas Quintae, 11 oct. 1949, Atchison, Kansas: The Abbey Student Press, St. Benedict's College [no date given].

THE ARCHDIOCESE OF LOS ANGELES

Constitutiones Latae et Promulgatae ab . . . Episcopo Montereyensi et Angelorum, in Synodo Dioecesana Prima, 4 maii. 1862, San Francisco: Ex Typis Vincentii Torras, 1862.

Constitutiones Latae et Promulgatae ab . . . Episcopo Montereyensi et Angelorum, in Synodo Dioecesana Secunda, 11-18 april. 1869, San Francisco: Ex Typis Mullin, Mahon, & Sociorum, 1869.

Constitutiones Latae et Promulgatae ab . . . Episcopo Montereyensi et Angelorum, in Synodo Quarta Dioecesana, 30, 31 iul. 1889, Los Angeles: Ex Typographia California Catholic, 1889.

Statuta Dioecesis Angelorum et Sancti Didaci Lata ac Promulgata . . . in Synodo Dioecesana Quinta, 6 dec. 1927, S. Ludovici: Typis B. Herder Book Co. [no date given].

THE ARCHDIOCESE OF LOUISVILLE

Constitutiones Dioecesis Ludovicopolitanae . . . in Synodo Dioecesana Prima . . . Latae et Promulgatae, 28-30 iul. 1850, Ludovicopoli: Typis Webb, M'Gill, et Levering, 1850.

Secunda Synodus Dioecesis Ludovicopolitanae, 1 sept. 1858 [no place or date of publication given].

Synodus Tertia Dioecesana Ludovicopolitana, 27 aug. 1862, Ludovicopoli: Typis Bradley et Gilbert, 1862.

Synodus Dioecesana Ludovicopolitana IV, 21 iul. 1874, Ludovicopoli: Excudebant Bradley & Gilbert, 1874.

Synodi Dioecesanae Ludovicopolitanae IV [21 iul. 1874], V [3 ian. 1889], VI [19 dec. 1894], VII [19 dec. 1902], Ludovicopoli, 1903.

THE ARCHDIOCESE OF NEWARK

Statuta Novarcensis Dioeceseos . . . in Synodo Dioecesana Prima . . . Lata et Promulgata, aug. 1856, Neo Eboraci: Edward Dunigan et Frater, 1857.

Statuta Novarcensis Dioeceseos . . . in Synodo Dioecesana Prima, mense augusto, 1856, Lata et Promulgata, iterumque, cum nonnulis Mutationibus Additionibusque, in Dioecesana Synodo, habita 10 iulii, 1868 . . . Confirmata, Novarce: Typis Societatis Pro Libris Catholicis Evulgandis, Neo Eboraci, 1869.

Statuta Dioecesis Novarcensis quae . . . in Synodo Dioecesana Tertia . . . Tulit et Promulgavit, 8-9 maii. 1878, Neo-Eboraci: Benziger Fratres, 1878.

Synodus Dioecesana Novarcensis Quinta, 17 nov. 1886, Arlington, Neo-Caes., Typis Paedotrophii SS. Cordis, 1887.

Statuta Dioecesis Novarcensis quae post Synodos Antecedentes, in Synodo Dioecesana Octava . . . Denuo Renovavit, Confirmavit et Promulgavit, 26 iun. 1896, Arlington, Neo-Caes.: Typis Paedotrophii SS. Cordis, 1897.

Statutes of the Archdiocese of Newark enacted and promulgated . . . in the First Archdiocesan Synod (Sixteenth of the Diocese of Newark), June 3, 1941, Arlington, N. J.: Catholic Protectory Press, 1941.

THE ARCHDIOCESE OF NEW ORLEANS

Synodus Dioecesana Neo-Aurelianensis Secunda, 21-28 april. 1844, Neo-Aureliae: Typis H. Meridier, 1844.

Synodus Dioecesana Neo-Aurelianensis Quarta, 26-28 ian. 1869, Neo-Aureliae: Ex Typis Propagatoris Catholici, 1869.

Synodus Dioecesana Neo-Aurelianensis Quinta, 3 maii. 1889, Neo-Aureliae: Ex Typis F. C. Philippe, 1889.

Constitutiones Dioeceseos Novae-Aureliae quae in Synodo Dioecesana Sexta . . . Latae et Promulgatae Fuerunt, 16 febr. 1922, New Orleans, Louisiana: Press of Sam W. Taylor [no date given].

THE ARCHDIOCESE OF NEW YORK

Synodus Dioecesana Neo-Eboracensis Prima, 28-31 aug. 1842, Neo-Eboraci: Typis Georgii Mitchell, 1842.

Synodus Dioecesana Neo-Eboracensis Secunda, 21 oct. 1848 [no place or date of publication given].

Synodus Dioecesana Neo-Eboracensis Tertia, 29 sept. 1868 [no place or date of publication given].

Synodus Dioecesana Neo-Eboracensis Quarta, 8, 9 nov. 1882, Neo-Eboraci: Typis Societatis Pro Libris Catholicis Evulgandis, 1882.

Synodus Dioecesana Neo-Eboracensis Quinta, 17, 18 nov. 1886, Neo-Eboraci: Typis Societatis Pro Libris Catholicis Evulgandis, 1886.

Synodus Dioecesana Neo-Eboracensis Sexta, 21 nov. 1889 [no place or date of publication given].

Synodus Dioecesana Neo-Eboracensis Septima, 23 nov. 1892 [no place or date of publication given].

Synodus Dioecesana Neo-Eboracensis Octava, 20 nov. 1895 [no place or date of publication given].

Synodus Dioecesana Neo-Eboracensis Nona, 23 nov. 1898 [no place or date of publication given].

Synodorum Archidioeceseos Neo-Eboracensis Collectio, Neo-Eboraci: Typis et Sumptibus Bibliothecae Cathedralis, 1901.

Acta et Statuta Synodi Neo-Eboracensis Decimae Septimae, 25 oct. 1950 [no place or date of publication given].

THE ARCHDIOCESE OF OMAHA

Synodus Dioecesana [Omahensis] Prima, 1, 2 mart. 1887, Philadelphiae: Ex Typographia Hardy et Mahony [no date given].

Statuta Dioecesana Synodorum Omahensium [Synodus Prima, 1 mart. 1887; Synodus Secunda, 27 iun. 1902], Omahae: Ex Typographia Burkley et Co. [no date given].

Synodus Dioecesana Omahensis Quarta, 14 iun. 1934, Omaha in Statu Nebraska: Typis Burkley Envelope & Printing Company, 1934.

THE ARCHDIOCESE OF PHILADELPHIA

Acta Synodi Dioecesanae Philadelphiensis Primae, 15 maii. 1832, Philadelphiae: Ex Typis F. Pierson, 1832.

Decreta Concilii Provincialis Philadelphiensis I, anno 1880 (Et Constitutiones Dioecesanae in Synodis Philadelphiensibus, annis 1832, 1842, 1847, 1853, 1855, 1857, 1886, et 1912 Latae et Promulgatae), Philadelphia, Pa.: Catholic Standard and Times Print [no date given].

Synodus Dioecesana Philadelphiensis IX, 26 april. 1934 [no place or date of publication given].

THE ARCHDIOCESE OF PORTLAND IN OREGON

Synodus Dioecesana Portlandensis in Oregon Tertia, 14 iun. 1935, Portland, Oregon: Sentinel Printery [no date given].

THE ARCHDIOCESE OF ST. LOUIS

Statuta Dioecesis Sti. Ludovici, Promulgata in Synodo Dioecesanâ Sancti Ludovicensi Prima, 21-28 april. 1839 [no place or date of publication available].

Statuta Lata et Promulgata ab . . . Archiepiscopo S. Ludovici, in Synodo, Dioecesana mense augusti, A.D. *1850 Habita,* S. Ludovici: Typis Ricardi Phillips, 1850.

Synodus Dioecesana Sti Ludovici Tertia, 8 sept. 1896, S. Ludovici: Apud Cancellariam Dioecesanam, 1897.

Synodus Dioecesana Sti Ludovici Quarta, 9 sept. 1902, Sti Ludovici: Apud Cancellariam Dioecesanam, 1902.

Synodus Dioecesana Sancti Ludovici Quinta, 3 oct. 1905, S. Ludovici: Cancellaria Dioecesana, 1905.

Synodus Dioecesana Sancti Ludovici Sexta, 26 iun. 1908, S. Ludovici: Cancellaria Dioecesana, 1908.

Synodus Dioecesana Sancti Ludovici Septima, 10 iun. 1929, Sancti Ludovici: Apud Cancellariam Dioecesanam [no date given].

Synodus Dioecesana Sancti Ludovici Octava, 10 maii. 1950 [no place or date of publication given].

THE ARCHDIOCESE OF ST. PAUL

Decreta Primae Synodi Dioecesanae . . . Sti. Pauli de Minnesota Habitae, 10 iun. 1861 [no place or date of publication given].

Decreta Secundae Synodi Dioecesanae . . . Sti. Pauli de Minnesota Habitae, 24 sept. 1863 [no place or date of publication given].

Decreta Tertiae Synodi Dioecesanae . . . Sti. Pauli de Minnesota Habitae, 14 iul. 1873 [no place or date of publication given].

Decreta Quartae Synodi Dioecesanae . . . Sti. Pauli de Minnesota Habitae, 24 aug. 1875 [no place or date of publication given].

THE ARCHDIOCESE OF SAN ANTONIO

Synodus Dioecesana Sti Antonii Secunda, 19 iul. 1906 [no place or date of publication given].

THE ARCHDIOCESE OF SAN FRANCISCO

Synodus Dioecesana [Prima] Sancti Francisci, 17 iul. 1862, Sancti Francisci: Ex Officinis Towne et Bacon, 1862.

Statuta Archidioecesis Sancti Francisci Lata ac Promulgata . . . in Synodo Dioecesana Secunda, 14 oct. 1936, San Francisco, California: Typis The Monitor Publishing Company [no date given].

THE ARCHDIOCESE OF SANTA FÉ

Constituciones Eclesiasticas para la Diocesis de Santa Fe N. M., Albuquerque, N. M.: Imprenta del Rio Grande, 1874.

Constitutiones Synodorum Dioecesanarum Sanctae Fidei Novi Mexici Primae [29 iun.–1 iul. 1888], Secundae [20, 21 aug. 1891] et Tertiae [28, 29 aug. 1893], Las Vegas, N. M.: Ex Typis "Revista Catolica," 1893.

THE ARCHDIOCESE OF SEATTLE

Acta et Statuta Synodi Dioecesis Nesqualiensis [sic] *I, 24-26 oct. 1883,* Tulalip, W. T.: Ex Typis Stae. Annae Missionis, 1884.

Synodus Dioecesana Nesquallienis Quarta, 8-9 aug. 1898, Portlandi, Oregon: Ex Typis Glass & Prudhomme, 1898.

Statuta Dioecesis Seattlensis Lata ac Promulgata . . . in Synodo Dioecesana Seattlensi Quinta, 1 iun. 1938, Seattle, Washington: Typis Metropolitan Press Printing Company [no date given].

DIOCESAN SYNODS

(The United States of America)

THE DIOCESE OF ALBANY

Dioeceseos Albanensis Statuta quae in Synodo Albanensi II . . . Lata ac Promulgata Fuere, 8-11 aug. 1869, Trojae, Neo-Eboraci: Excudebant Albert W. Scribner et Socii, 1869.

Synodus Dioecesana Albanensis Tertia, 6-7 febr. 1884, Neo-Eboraci: Typis "Catholic Publication Society Co.," 1884.

Synodus Dioecesana Albanensis Quarta, Synodus Superiores Mutans et Agens, 19 iul. 1887, Trojae: Excudebat T. J. Hurley, 1887.

Synodus Dioecesana Albanensis Quinta, 2 dec. 1890, Trojae: Excudebat T. J. Hurley, 1890.

Statuta Dioecesis Albanensis in Sexta Synodo Dioecesana . . . Promulgata et Edita, 31 ian. 1895, Albaniae: Excudebant Weed-Parsons Sociique, Typographi, 1895.

Statuta Dioecesis Albanensis in Septima Synodo Dioecesana . . . Promulgata et Edita, 4 ian. 1898, Albaniae: Excudebant Weed-Parsons Sociique, Typographi, 1898.

Statuta Dioecesis Albanensis in Octava Synodo Dioecesana . . . Promulgata et Edita, 16 ian. 1901, Albaniae: Excudebant Weed-Parsons Sociique, Typographi, 1901.

THE DIOCESE OF ALEXANDRIA

Synodus Dioecesana Natchitochensis Secunda, 14-15 febr. 1869, Neo-Aureliae: Ex Typis Propagatoris Catholici, 1869.

Statuta Dioeceses [sic] *Alexandrinae quae in Synodo Dioecesana Quarta . . . Sanxit et Promulgavit, 30 nov. 1921,* Alexandria: Ex Typis "Wall Printing Co.," 1922.

The Diocese of Altoona–Johnstown

Synodus Altunensis Prima, 29 nov. 1922, Lancaster, Pa.: Wickersham Printing Co., 1923.

The Diocese of Atlanta

(*Cf. The Diocese of Savannah*)

The Diocese of Belleville

Synodus Dioecesana Bellevillensis Secunda, 15 iun. 1904, Belleville, Illinois: Buechler Printing Company [no date given].

Synodus Dioecesana Bellevillensis Tertia, 19 nov. 1909, Belleville, Illinois: Buechler Printing Company, 1909.

Synodus Dioecesana Bellevillensis Quarta, 1 dec. 1920, Belleville, Ill.: Buechler Printing Co. [no date given].

Statuta Dioecesis Bellevillensis Lata ac Promulgata . . . in Synodo Dioecesana Bellevillensi Quinta, 27 dec. 1939, Belleville, Illinois: Buechler Printing Co., 1940.

The Diocese of Bismarck

First Diocesan Synod of the Diocese of Bismarck, Nov. 12, 1924 [no place or date of publication given].

The Diocese of Boise

Statuta Dioecesis Xylopolitanae Lata ac Promulgata . . . in Synodo Dioecesana Xylopolitana Secunda, 20 iun. 1941, Boise, Idaho: Syms-York Company [no date given].

The Diocese of Brooklyn

Statuta Synodi Brooklynensis [sic] *Primae, 29 aug. 1879,* Neo-Eboraci: Ex Typis H. J. Hewitt, 1880.

Constitutiones Dioecesanae Brooklynienses [sic] *quas in Synodo Dioecesana Tertia . . . Sanxit et Promulgavit, 27 dec. 1894,* Neo-Eboraci: Typis Missionis Virginis Immaculatae, 1895.

Constitutiones Dioecesanae Brooklynienses [sic] *quas in Synodo Dioecesana Quinta . . . Sanxit et Promulgavit, 25-26 febr. 1926,* New York: Press of Loughlin Bros. [no date given].

The Diocese of Buffalo

Statuta Dioeceseos Buffalensis in Decretis Emendatis ex Synodis A.D. 1847, 1849, 1850, 1852, 1854, 1855, 1856, 1857, 1859, 1860, 1861, 1862, et 1863 Habitis [no place or date of publication given].

Synodus Dioecesana Buffalensis Secunda, 17-19 iun. 1849, Buffalo: Typis Brunck & Domedion, 1850.

Statuta Dioecesis Buffalensis Lata in Synodo Dioecesana [*Quinta*], *anno 1854,* Buffalo: Typis Wieckmann & Brandt, 1854.

Synodus Dioecesana Buffalensis Decima Septima, 13 aug. 1871, Buffalensi, 1871.

Synodus Dioecesana Buffalensis Vigesima, quae Complectitur etiam Statuta Lata in Synodis ab A.D. 1847 usque ad 1879, 30 nov.–2 dec. 1886, Buffalone: Typis Courier Company, 1886.

Synodus Dioecesana Buffalensis Vigesima Prima, 10 iun. 1891, Buffalone, N. Eb.: Typis Soc. Cath. Publ. [no date given].

Synodus Dioecesana Buffalensis Vigesima Secunda, 6 iun. 1894, Buffalone, N. Eb.: Typis Soc. Cath. Publ. [no date given].

Synodus Dioecesana Buffalensis Vigesima Tertia, 30 iun. 1897, Buffalone, N. Eb.: Typis Soc. Cath. Publ. [no date given].

Synodus Dioecesana Buffalensis Vigesima Quarta, 30 oct. 1901, Buffalone, N. Eb.: Typis Soc. Cath. Publ., 1901.

Synodus Dioecesana Buffalensis Vigesima Septima, 14 maii. 1924, Buffalo: The Union and Times Press [no date given].

Synodus Dioecesana Buffalensis Duodetricesima, 9 nov. 1938, Buffalo: Union and Times Press [no date given].

The Diocese of Burlington

Statuta Dioecesis Burlingtonensis, St. Albans: Advertiser Printing House, 1878.

Statuta Dioecesis Burlingtonensis, anno 1886, Burlington, Vt., 1886.

Statuta Dioecesis Burlingtonensis, 24 iun. 1907, Boston: Angel Guardian Press, 1907.

The Diocese of Camden

Synodus Dioecesana Camdensis Prima, 17 maii. 1955, Philadelphia, Pa.: Press of Jefferies and Manz, Inc. [no date given].

The Diocese of Charleston

The Constitution of the Roman Catholic Churches of the States of North Carolina, South Carolina and Georgia; which are Comprised in the Diocess [sic] *of Charleston, and the Province of Baltimore, U.S.A.,* 2. ed., Dec. 31, 1839, Charleston: Burges & James, 1840.

Statuta quae in Synodo Carolopolitana XVI. Lata ac Promulgata Fuere, Carolopoli: Excudebant Walker, Evans & Cogswell et Socii [no date given].

Constitutiones Dioecesanae Carolopolitanae, quas in Synodo Dioecesana Septima Decima . . . Habita, 21 april. 1925, Charleston: J. J. Furlong & Son, Charleston Printing House [no date given].

The Diocese of Cheyenne

Statuta Dioecesana (Ex Synodis Dioeceseos Omahensis Sumpta) Lata in Synodo Prima Cheyennensi, 17 april. 1923, Omahae, Nebr.: Ex Typographia Swartz Print Co. [no date given].

Statutes of the Diocese of Cheyenne Enacted and Promulgated . . . in the Second Diocesan Synod, June 11, 1948, Cheyenne, Wyo.: Wyoming Labor Journal Publishing Co. [no date given].

THE DIOCESE OF CLEVELAND

Constitutiones Dioecesis Clevelandensis quae in Synodis Dioecesanis A.D. 1852, 1854, 1857, 1868 Habitis Edictae Sunt, Clevelandi, 1869.

Statuta Dioecesis Clevelandensis, in Synodis Dioecesanis, habitis Annis Domini 1852, 1854, 1857, 1868, 1872, 1882, Lata et, prout nunc Prostant, Edita in Synodo [Sexta], die 27 mensis maii, A.D. 1882, Clevelandi: M. E. M'Cabe, Typographus, 1882.

Acta et Statuta VII Synodi Dioecesanae Clevelandensis Habitae die 3, Januarii 1889 [no place or date of publication given].

THE DIOCESE OF COLUMBUS

Record of the Second Diocesan Synod of Columbus, August 27, 1873, Columbus, Ohio: Nevins & Myers, 1873.

Synodus Dioecesana Columbensis Quarta, 16 iul. 1902 [no place or date of publication given].

Fifth Synod of the Diocese of Columbus, October 8, 1952 [no place or date of publication given].

THE DIOCESE OF COVINGTON

Acta et Constitutiones Synodi Dioecesanae Covingtoniensis [sic] *Primae, 10-12 sept. 1879,* Cincinnati, O.: Fr. Pustet & Co., 1880.

Acta et Decreta Synodi Dioecesanae Covingtonensis Secundae, 28-30 sept. 1886, Cincinnati: Typis Braunwart & Brockhoff, 1886.

Acta et Decreta Synodi Dioecesanae Covingtonensis Tertiae, 20 mart. 1934, Covington, Ky.: The Messenger Press, 1934.

THE DIOCESE OF CROOKSTON

Statutes of the Diocese of Crookston Promulgated at the Diocesan Synod held September 20, 1921, St. Louis, Mo.: B. Herder Book Co., 1923.

THE DIOCESE OF DAVENPORT

Synodus Dioecesana Davenportensis Secunda, 22 iun. 1904 [no place or date of publication given].

Statutes [*of the*] *Third Synod* [*of the*] *Diocese of Davenport, June 7, 1932* [no place or date of publication given].

THE DIOCESE OF DES MOINES

The Code of the Diocese of Des Moines Decreed in Diocesan Synod held June 15th, 1923 [no place or date of publication given].

Dioecesis Des Moinensis Synodus Dioecesana Tertia, 16 iun. 1933, Des Moines, Iowa: Burken Printing Company [no date given].

THE DIOCESE OF DODGE CITY

The Statutes of the Diocese of Dodge City, as promulgated by His Excellency, the Most Reverend John B. Franz, Bishop of Dodge City, in the Pro-Synodal Decree of September 12, 1952 [no place or date of publication given].

THE DIOCESE OF DULUTH

Statutes of the Diocese of Duluth, Collegeville, Minnesota: Record Press, St. John's University [no date given; however, the *Imprimatur* was issued July 1, 1912].

THE DIOCESE OF ERIE

Statuta Dioecesis Eriensis Lata in Synodo Dioecesana Celebrata A.D. 1855 et in alia Synodo A.D. 1868, Erie: Ex Officinis "Observatoris," 1869.

Statuta Dioeceseos Eriensis . . . Promulgata in Synodo Dioecesana Sexta, 9 maii. 1912 [no place or date of publication given].

Synodus Dioecesana Eriensis Septima, 29 oct. 1942 [no place or date of publication given].

THE DIOCESE OF EVANSVILLE

Statuta Dioecesis Evansvicensis Lata ac Promulgata . . . in Synodo Dioecesana Prima, 11 oct. 1948, Evansville, Ind.: Typis Moser Printing Co. [no date given].

THE DIOCESE OF FALL RIVER

Statuta Dioecesis Riverormensis quae in Synodo Dioecesana Prima . . . Sanxit et Promulgavit, 28 iun. 1905, Philadelphia: Ex Typis the Dolphin Press, 1905.

THE DIOCESE OF FARGO

Synodus Dioecesana Fargensis Prima, 29-30 sept. 1941, Milwauchiae: Ex Typographia Bruce, 1941.

Synodus Dioecesana Fargensis Secunda, 2-3 oct. 1951, Milwauchiae: Ex Typographia Bruce, 1951.

THE DIOCESE OF FORT WAYNE–SOUTH BEND

Statutes for the Administration of the Temporal Affairs of the Congregations within the Diocese of Fort Wayne, Promulgated in Synod, August 26, 1863, Cincinnati: John P. Walsh, 1863.

Statutes for the Government of the Clergy within the Diocese of Fort Wayne, Promulgated in Conference of the Clergy at Notre Dame University, July 15, 1866, Notre Dame, Ind.: Ave Maria Steam Power Press [no date given].

Statuta Dioecesis Wayne Castrensis in Synodo Diocesana [sic] [*25, 26 oct.*] *1874 Promulgata,* Fort Wayne: Sentinel Steam Printing House, 1875.

Statuta Dioecesis Wayne Castrensis in Synodis Dioecesanis 1874 et Annis Sequentibus [1882, 1884, 1886] Promulgata, Fort Wayne, Ind.: W. D. Page, Printer and Publisher, 1892.

Synodus Dioecesana Wayne-Castrensis, 11 nov. 1903, Nostrae Dominae, Indiana: Typis Universitatis [no date given].

Synodus Dioecesana Wayne Castrensis habita die 19 augusti 1926 [no place or date of publication given].

THE DIOCESE OF GALVESTON–HOUSTON

Synodus Dioecesana Galvestonensis [sic] *Prima, 13-20 iun. 1858,* Neo-Aureliae: Ex Typis Propagatoris Catholici, 1858.

Synodus Gemina Dioecesana Galvestonensis [sic] *Secunda . . . in Civitate Galvestonensi 14-18 dec. 1868 et in Civitate Sti Antonii 4 ian. 1869 Habita,* Neo-Aureliae: Ex Typis Propagatoris Catholici, 1869.

Synodus Dioecesana Galvestoniensis Septima, 23 april. 1930 [no place or date of publication given].

THE DIOCESE OF GRAND RAPIDS

Synodus Dioecesana Grandormensis Prima, 18 sept. 1903 [no place or date of publication given].

THE DIOCESE OF GREAT FALLS

Synodus Dioecesana Greatormensis Prima, 21 iun. 1935, Portland, Oregon: Sentinel Printery [no date given].

THE DIOCESE OF GREEN BAY

Decreta edita in Synodo Dioecesana Prima celebrata Sinu Viridi . . . diebus 11mo et 12mo julii, A.D. 1876, Sinu Viridi, Wis.: Robinson Brothers & Clark, Printers, 1877.

Statuta Synodi Dioecesanae Sinus Viridis Secundae, 21-23 maii. 1889, Green Bay, Wis.: Ex Typographia Landsmann, 1890.

Statuta Dioecesis Sinus Viridis [Synodus III], anno 1898, Green Bay, Wis.: Ex Typographia Landsmann, 1898.

Constitutiones Dioeceseos Synus [sic] *Viridis . . . quae in Synodo Dioecesana Quarta . . . Latae et Promulgatae Fuerunt, 14-16 dec. 1920,* Pulaski, Wisc.: Typis Franciscanae Typographiae [no date given].

THE DIOCESE OF HARRISBURG

Synodus Harrisburgensis Secunda, 27, 28 iun. 1893, Baltimorae: Typis Foley Fratrum, 1893.

Statuta Dioecesis Harrisburgensis quae in Synodo Dioecesana Sexta . . . Sanxit et Promulgavit, 28 sept. 1911, Philadelphia, Pa.: The Dolphin Press, 1911.

Synodus Dioecesana Harrisburgensis Octava, 17 ian. 1928, Philadelphia: Ex Typis Dolphin Press, 1928.

Ninth Synod of the Diocese of Harrisburg, Dec. 16, 1943 [no place or date of publication given].

THE DIOCESE OF KANSAS CITY–ST. JOSEPH

Synodus Dioecesana Kansanopolitana Prima, 14-16 iun. 1887, Baltimorae: Excudebant Foley Fratres, 1887.

Decreta Synodi Dioecesanae Kansanopolitanae Secundae, 9 april. 1912, Atchison, Kans.: Abbey Student Press, St. Benedict's College, 1912.

Statuta Dioecesana, Decreta Synodi Dioecesanae Kansanopolitanae Tertiae, 20 april. 1920, Atchison, Kansas: Abbey Student Press [no date given].

Synodus Dioecesana Kansanopolitana Quarta, 30 oct. 1928 [no place or date of publication given].

Diocesan Statutes, Fifth Synod, Kansas City, Missouri, Dec. 14, 1948 [no place or date of publication given].

Statuta ab . . . Dom. Joanne Josepho Hogan, Episcopo Sti Josephi, in Synodo Dioecesana . . . Lata et Promulgata, 11, 12 febr. 1879, Sti Josephi, Mo.: Ex Typis Jo. H. McGuire, 1879.

Statuta Dioecesana quae in Synodo Tertia S. Joseph . . . Lata et Promulgata Fuerunt, 27 ian. 1930, Sancti Joseph: Apud Cancellariam Dioecesanam, 1930.

THE DIOCESE OF LA CROSSE

Constitutiones Dioeceseos Crossensis, contained in *Decreta Synodi Milwauchiensis Primae, anno 1857 habitae, etiam in Dioecesibus Sinus Viridi et Crossensi Obligatoria*, Milwauchiae: Typis P. V. Deuster, 1869.

Statuta Recentiora die 6to mens. julii 1864 promulgata a Reverendissimo Joanne Martine Henni, Episcopo Milwauchiensi, ac pariter in Dioecesibus Sinus Viridi et Crossensi Obligatoria [no place or date of publication given].

Decreta Synodi Dioecesanae Crossensis I, 25, 26 iul. 1871, Milwauchiae: Excudebat P. V. Deuster, 1871.

Synodus Dioecesana Grossensis Secunda, 24, 25 aug. 1887, Milwaukiae: Eduardi Keough, 1888.

Third Synod of the Diocese of La Crosse, April 27, 1955, La Crosse, Wisc.: G. A. Keller Print [no date given].

THE DIOCESE OF LAFAYETTE

Constitutiones Dioeceseos Lafayettensis in Synodo Dioecesana Prima . . . Latae et Promulgatae, 16 iun. 1923 [no place or date of publication given].

Constitutions of the Diocese of Lafayette Promulgated . . . at the Second Diocesan Synod, October 18, 1933 [no place or date of publication given].

Constitutions of the Diocese of Lafayette Promulgated . . . at the Third

Diocesan Synod held October 8, 1943 [no place or date of publication given].

Fourth Diocesan Synod of the Diocese of Lafayette, Dec. 28, 1953 [no place or date of publication given].

THE DIOCESE OF LINCOLN

Statutes of the Diocese of Lincoln Promulgated at the First Diocesan Synod, June 4, 1934 [no place or date of publication given].

THE DIOCESE OF LITTLE ROCK

Synodus Dioecesana Petriculana Prima, 16 febr. 1909, Petriculae: Apud Cancellariam Dioecesanam, 1909.

THE DIOCESE OF MADISON

First Synod of the Diocese of Madison, Celebrated February 22, 1956, Madison, Wisconsin: Cantwell Printing Co., 1956.

THE DIOCESE OF MANCHESTER

Constitutiones Dioecesanae ab . . . Episcopo Manchesteriensi in Synodo Dioecesana Prima . . . Latae et Promulgatae, 4 nov. 1886, Manchester, N. H.: Typis Ormond D. Kimball, 1886.

THE DIOCESE OF MARQUETTE

Statuta Dioecesis Sanctae Mariae, Cincinnati: Typis Caleb Clark, 1856.

Statuta Dioecesis Marianopolitanae in Michigan, Detroiti: Ex Typis Joannis Slater, 1863.

Synodus Dioecesana Marianopol. et Marquettensis Secunda, 21 iul. 1905, Techny, Illinois: The Society of the Divine Word, 1906.

Synodus Dioecesana Marquettensis Tertia, 5 dec. 1950 [no place or date of publication given].

THE DIOCESE OF MOBILE–BIRMINGHAM

Decreta Synodi Mobiliensis Primae, 19 ian. 1835, Notre Dame, Indiana: University Press, 1890.

Statuta Synodi Mobiliensis Primae, 18 nov. 1861 [*sic,* titled the First Synod, although one had previously been held in 1835], Montgomery, Ala.: Montgomery Advertiser Book & Job Office, 1862. Also published at Mobile: Spring Hill College, 1868.

Synodus Mobiliensis Secunda, 10 aug. 1888, Mobile, Ala.: Daily Register Print, 1888.

Decreta Synodi Dioecesanae Mobiliensis Tertiae, 24 iun. 1921, Mobile, Ala.: Ex Typographia Patterson Printing Co., Inc. [no date given].

THE DIOCESE OF MONTEREY–FRESNO

Statuta Dioecesis Montereyensis-Fresnensis . . . in Prima Synodo Dioece-

sana . . . Lata et Promulgata, 29, 30 oct. 1929, Fresni: Sumptibus Saint Columba Guild, Typis Crown Printing [no date given].

THE DIOCESE OF NASHVILLE

Synodus Dioecesana Nashvillensis Prima, 10 febr. 1905 [no place or date of publication given].

The Third Synod of the Diocese of Nashville, Sept. 16, 1947 [no place or date of publication given].

THE DIOCESE OF NATCHEZ–JACKSON

Synodus Dioecesana Natchetensis Prima, 16-18 april. 1858, Neo-Aureliae: Ex Typis Propagatoris Catholici, 1858.

Acta et Constitutiones Synodi Dioecesanae Natchetensis, 22 ian. 1862 [no place or date of publication given].

Synodus Dioecesana Natchetensis Quarta, 19-21 ian. 1874 [no place or date of publication given].

Synodus Dioecesana Natchetensis Quinta, 16, 17 sept. 1886 [no place or date of publication given].

Synodus Dioecesana Natchetensis Sexta, 26 april. 1892 [no place or date of publication given].

Synodus Dioecesana Natchetensis Septima, 27 april.–5 maii. 1897 [no place or date of publication given].

Constitutiones Dioeceseos Natchetensis quae in Synodo Dioecesana Octava . . . Latae et Promulgatae Fuerunt, 14 iul. 1922, New Orleans: Sam W. Taylor, Service Printery [no date given].

Acta Synodi Dioecesanae Natchetensis Nonae, 9-11 iul. 1935 [no place or date of publication given].

Tenth Diocesan Synod of the Diocese of Natchez-Jackson, May 23, 1957 [no place or date of publication given].

THE DIOCESE OF OGDENSBURG

Statuta Dioeceseos Ogdensburgensis quae in Synodo Ogdensburgensi I . . . Lata ac Promulgata Fuere, 13, 14 iul. 1875, Troy, N. Y.: Excudebat T. J. Hurley, 1875.

Statuta Dioeceseos Ogdensburgensis quae in Synodo Ogdensburgensi II . . . Lata ac Promulgata Fuere, anno 1886, Troy, N. Y.: Excudebat T. J. Hurley, 1886.

Synodus Ogdensburgensis Quarta (Supplementum Synodo IIae), 25 oct. 1892, Ogdensburg: Excudebat Republican & Journal Co., 1893.

Synodus Ogdensburgensis Sexta (Supplementum Synodo IIae), 20 oct. 1898, Ogdensburg: Excudebat Republican & Journal Co., 1898.

Synodus Ogdensburgensis Septima (Supplementum Synodo IIae), 22 oct. 1901, Ogdensburg: Excudebat Republican & Journal Co., 1901.

Statuta Dioecesis Ogdensburgensis quae in Synodo Ogdensburgensi VIII, A.D. 1904, Lata ac Promulgata Fuere, Ogdensburg: Republican & Journal Company, 1905.

THE DIOCESE OF OKLAHOMA CITY AND TULSA

Statuta Dioeceseos Oklahomensis quae in Synodo Prima . . . Sanxit et Promulgavit, 21 aug. 1913, Ex Typis Orphanotropii Sancti Josephi, Apud Oklahomam, in Oklahoma [no date given].

THE DIOCESE OF OWENSBORO

The First Synod of the Diocese of Owensboro, February 22, 1943 [no place or date of publication given].

THE DIOCESE OF PEORIA

Constitutiones Dioecesis Peoriensis quae in Synodo Dioecesana Tertia . . . Latae et Promulgatae Fuerunt, 1 dec. 1915, Bloomington, Illinois: Typis Pantagraph Printing and Stationery Co., 1915.

Statutes of the Fourth Synod of the Diocese of Peoria, Dec. 19, 1944 [no place or date of publication given].

THE DIOCESE OF PITTSBURGH

Statuta Dioecesis Pittsburgensis Lata in Synodo Dioecesana [Prima] habita A.D. 1844, cum Decretis in aliis Synodis A.D. 1846, 1854, 1858, et 1869, Promulgatis, Pittsburgi: Ex Typographia Jacobi Porter, 1870.

Decreta Edita in Synodo IVa Pittsburgensi, 12 aug. 1858 [no place or date of publication given].

Decreta Edita in Synodo Va [Pittsburgensi], anno 1869 [no place or date of publication given].

Statuta Dioeceseos Pittsburgensis . . . Promulgata in Synodo Dioecesana Sexta, 7-9 febr. 1893, Pittsburgi: Rawsthorne Engraving and Printing Co., 1893.

Statuta Synodi Septimae Pittsburgensis, 16 april. 1896 [no place or date of publication given].

Decreta Synodi Octavae Pittsburgensis, 13 oct. 1899 [no place or date of publication given].

Decreta Synodi Nonae Pittsburgensis, 30 oct. 1902 [no place or date of publication given].

Statuta Dioeceseos Pittsburgensis in Synodo Dioecesanis Lata, et prout nunc prostant Promulgata in Synodo Dioecesana Decima, 10 oct. 1905 [no place or date of publication given].

Statuta Dioeceseos Pittsburgensis . . . Promulgata in Synodo Dioecesana Decima Quarta, 8 oct. 1919, Pittsburgh: St. Joseph's Protectory Print, 1920.

THE DIOCESE OF PORTLAND

Acta et Decreta Secundae Synodi Dioecesis Portlandensis, 1 iul. 1904, Romae: Typis Vaticanis, 1905.

THE DIOCESE OF PROVIDENCE

Acta et Decreta Synodi Dioecesanae Providentiensis Tertiae, 21 dec. 1887, Woodstock: Ex Typis Collegii Woodstockiensis, 1888.

THE DIOCESE OF PUEBLO

Statutes of the Diocese of Pueblo Enacted and Promulgated . . . in the First Diocesan Synod, August 25, 1948 [no place or date of publication given].

THE DIOCESE OF RALEIGH

First Synod of the Diocese of Raleigh, April 26, 1948 [no place or date of publication given].

THE DIOCESE OF RICHMOND

Statuta Synodi Richmondensis [sic] *Primae, 14, 15 oct. 1856,* Baltimori: Apud Joannem Murphy et Socios, 1857.

Acta et Statuta Synodi Richmondensis [sic] *Secundae, 18-20 aug. 1886,* Baltimorae: Excudebant Joannes Murphy et Socii, 1886.

Synodus Dioecesana Richmondiensis Tertia, 16 febr. 1933, Richmond, Virginia: Lewis Printing Company, Inc. [no date given].

THE DIOCESE OF ROCHESTER

Acta et Statuta Synodi Dioecesanae Roffensis Primae, 13, 14 oct. 1875, Roffae: Ex Typis Union and Advertiser Company, 1875.

Statuta Dioecesana . . . in Synodo Roffensi Secunda . . . Lata et Promulgata, 14 iun. 1887, Roffae: Ex Typis Union and Advertiser, 1887.

Acta Synodi Roffensis Tertiae, 9 iun. 1914, Rochester: Typis Joannis P. Smith Printing Co., 1914.

Synodus Roffensis Quinta, 12 dec. 1934, Rochester: Art Print Shop, 1935.

THE DIOCESE OF ROCKFORD

Synodus Dioecesana Rockfordensis [sic] *Prima, 4 april. 1916,* Chicagine: Praelo Commiserunt Mayer et Miller Socii, 1916.

THE DIOCESE OF SACRAMENTO

Synodus Dioecesana Sacramentensis [*Prima*], *24 oct. 1887,* Sancti Francisci: Typis P. J. Thomas, 1887.

THE DIOCESE OF ST. AUGUSTINE

Synodus Dioecesana I Sancti Augustini, 19 oct. 1861 [no place or date of publication available].

Synodus Dioecesana III Sancti Augustini, 10 dec. 1902, St. Augustine, Fla.: Record [no date given].

THE DIOCESE OF ST. CLOUD

Synodal Decrees of the Diocese of Saint Cloud Promulgated in [*the First*] *Diocesan Synod, June 10, 1924* [no place or date of publication given].

Additions and Amendments to the Synodal Decrees of the Diocese of St. Cloud Promulgated in the [*Second*] *Diocesan Synod held June 20, 1929* [no place or date of publication given].

Synodal Decrees of the Diocese of Saint Cloud Promulgated in the Third Diocesan Synod, June 22, 1939 [no place or date of publication given].

THE DIOCESE OF SALT LAKE CITY

Statuta Dioecesis Lacus Salsi Lata ac Promulgata . . . in Synodo Dioecesana Prima, 17 iun. 1929, Bronx, N. Y.: New York Catholic Protectory [no date given].

THE DIOCESE OF SAN DIEGO

Statutes of the Diocese of San Diego, First Diocesan Synod, February 24, 1943, amended, 1949 [no place or date of publication given].

THE DIOCESE OF SAVANNAH
(THE DIOCESE OF ATLANTA)

Statuta Dioecesis Savannensis . . . in Synodo Dioecesana Sexta . . . Lata et Promulgata, 11 sept. 1879 [no place or date of publication given].

Constitutiones Dioecesanae Savannensis, quas in Synodo Dioecesana Octava . . . Confirmavit et Auxit, 12 iul. 1900, Neo Eboraci: Typis Caroli A. Searing, 1900.

Statuta Dioecesis Savannensis-Atlantensis necnon Facultates Sacerdotibus Concessae, 30 maii. 1939, Savannah, Georgia: Chancery Office, 1939.

THE DIOCESE OF SCRANTON

First Synod of the Diocese of Scranton, May 4, 1949 [no place or date of publication given].

THE DIOCESE OF SIOUX CITY

Acta Synodi Sioupolitanae Primae, 22 aug. 1902 [no place or date of publication given].

Synodus Dioecesana Sioupolitana Secunda, 6 ian. 1909, Philadelphia, Pa.: The Dolphin Press, 1909.

Synodus Dioecesana Sioupolitana Tertia, 10 ian. 1912 [no place or date of publication given].

Statuta Dioecesana Facta et Promulgata in Quarta Synodo . . . Dioecesis Sioupolitanae, 24 nov. 1931, Ex Cancellaria Dioecesana, 1931.

Synodus Dioecesana Sioupolitana Quinta, 25 nov. 1941 [no place or date of publication given].

THE DIOCESE OF SIOUX FALLS

Synodus Dioecesana Siouxormensis Tertia, 27 ian. 1949, Sioux Falls, S. D.: Diocese of Sioux Falls, 1949.

THE DIOCESE OF SPOKANE

Statuta Dioecesis Spokanensis Lata ac Promulgata . . . in Synodo Dioecesana Spokanensi Prima, 13 april. 1939, Seattle, Washington: Typis Metropolitan Press Printing Company [no date given].

THE DIOCESE OF SPRINGFIELD

Constitutiones Dioecesanae ab . . . Episcopo Campifontis in Synodo Dioecesana Prima habita Campifonte [29 ian.] A.D. 1874, Latae et Promulgatae, Worcester: Press of Charles Hamilton, 1881.

THE DIOCESE OF SPRINGFIELD IN ILLINOIS

Synodus Dioecesana Altonensis Prima, 27 febr. 1889, S. Ludovici: Typis "Amerika," 1889.

Acta et Statuta Synodi Secundae Campifontis in Illinois, 10 mart. 1953 [no place or date of publication given].

THE DIOCESE OF SYRACUSE

Synodus Dioecesana Syracusana Prima, 14 sept. 1887, Neo-Eboraci: Typis Societatis Pro Libris Catholicis Evulgandis, 1887.

Synodus Dioecesana Syracusana Secunda, 30 sept. 1890, Syracusis, in Statu Neo-Eboracensi: Catholic Sun Press, 1890.

Synodus Dioecesana Syracusana Tertia, 6 nov. 1893, Syracusis, in Statu Neo-Eboracensi, 1893.

Synodus Dioecesana Syracusana Quarta, 22 oct. 1896, Syracusis, in Statu Neo-Eboracensi, 1896.

Synodus Dioecesana Syracusana Quinta, 18 oct. 1899, Syracusis, in Statu Neo-Eboracensi, 1899.

Synodus Dioecesana Syracusana Septima, 17 oct. 1905, Syracusis, in Statu Neo-Eboracensi: Catholic Sun Press, 1905.

Synodus Dioecesana Syracusana Octava, 13 oct. 1908, Syracusis, in Statu Neo-Eboracensi: Catholic Sun Press, 1908.

Synodus Dioecesana Syracusensis Undecima, 8 sept. 1921, Rochester, N. Y.: Typis Joannis P. Smith Printing Co., 1922.

THE DIOCESE OF TOLEDO

Acta et Decreta Synodi Dioecesanae Toletanae Primae, 4 nov. 1941, Toleti: Cancellaria Curiae Dioecesanae, 1941.

THE DIOCESE OF TRENTON

Statuta Dioeceseos Trentonensis, quae in Synodo Dioecesana Secunda . . .

Sanxit et Promulgavit, 25 iun. 1896, Trentonii: Typis "True American," 1897.

Synodus Dioecesana Trentonensis Tertia, 9 iun. 1931 [no place or date of publication given].

THE DIOCESE OF TUCSON

Synodus Dioecesana Vicariatus Apostolici Arizonensis Prima, 29 ian. 1892, Tucson: Excudebat the Citizen Printing and Publishing Company, 1892.

Statuta Dioecesis Tucsonensis . . . in Synodo Dioecesana Secunda . . . Lata ac Promulgata, 30 nov. 1928, Typis Tucsonensibus F. H. Keddington Co., 1928.

THE DIOCESE OF WHEELING

Statuta ab . . . Episcopo Wheelingensi [sic], *in Synodo Dioecesana . . . Lata et Promulgata, 28, 29 oct. 1873,* Wheeling: Ex Typis Jacobi F. Carroll, 1873.

Synodus Dioecesana Wheelingensis [sic] *Quarta, 9, 10 aug. 1882,* Wheelingii: Excudebat Jacobus F. Carroll, Typographus, 1882.

Synodus Dioecesana Wheelingensis [sic] *Quinta, 7, 8 aug. 1888,* Wheelingii: Excudebat Jacobus F. Carroll Typographus, 1888.

Statutes of the Diocese of Wheeling Promulgated at the [*VII*] *Diocesan Synod held May 15, 1923* [no place or date of publication given].

THE DIOCESE OF WILMINGTON

Synodus Dioecesana Wilmingtonensis [sic] *Prima, 9 april. 1879,* Wilmington, Del.: Excudebant Glatts & Eckel, 1879.

Statuta Dioeceseos Wilmingtoniensis quae in Synodo Dioecesana Tertia . . . Sanxit et Promulgavit, 17 nov. 1898, Baltimorae, Md.: Excudebant Foley Fratres, 1898.

THE DIOCESE OF WINONA

Statutes of the Diocese of Winona Enacted and Promulgated . . . in the First Diocesan Synod, June 15, 1950 [no place or date of publication given].

REFERENCE WORKS

Abbo, John A.–Hannan, Jerome D., *The Sacred Canons,* 2 vols., St. Louis: B. Herder Book Co., 1952.

Aquinas, St. Thomas, *Summa Theologica,* 4 vols., Taurini: Marietti, 1948.

Augustine, Charles, *A Commentary on the New Code of Canon Law,* 8 vols., Vol. VI, 2. ed., St. Louis: B. Herder Book Co., 1923.

———, *Liturgical Law,* St. Louis: B. Herder Book Co., 1931.

Barrett, John Daniel Mary, *A Comparative Study of the Councils of Baltimore and the Code of Canon Law,* The Catholic University of America

Canon Law Studies, n. 83, Washington, D. C.: The Catholic University of America, 1932.

Beste, Udalricus, *Introductio in Codicem,* 3. ed., Collegeville, Minn.: St. John's Abbey Press, 1946.

Bouscaren, T. Lincoln–Ellis, Adam C., *Canon Law, A Text and Commentary,* Milwaukee: The Bruce Publishing Company, 1949.

Cappello, Felix M., *Summa Iuris Canonici,* 3 vols., Vols. I, II, 5. ed., Romae: Apud Aedes Universitatis Gregorianae, 1951.

———, *Tractatus Canonico-Moralis de Sacramentis,* 5 vols., Vol. I, 6. ed., Taurini: Marietti, 1953.

Catholic Encyclopedia, The, 15 vols. and 2 supplements, New York: Robert Appleton Co., 1907-1922.

Cicognani, Amleto, *Canon Law,* 2. ed., Westminster, Maryland: The Newman Press, 1949.

Coronata, Matthaeus Conte a, *Institutiones Iuris Canonici,* 5 vols., Vol. I, 4. ed., 1950, Vol. II, 4. ed., 1951, Taurini: Marietti.

Donnelly, Francis Bernard, *The Diocesan Synod,* The Catholic University of America Canon Law Studies, n. 74, Washington, D. C.: The Catholic University of America, 1932.

Feldhaus, Aloysius H., *Oratories,* The Catholic University of America Canon Law Studies, n. 42, Washington, D. C.: The Catholic University of America, 1927.

Gasquet, Abbot, *Parish Life in Mediaeval England,* New York: Benziger Brothers, 1906.

Gilmour, Richard, *Rules and Directions for the Administration of the Temporal and Spiritual Affairs of Churches, Schools, etc., in the Diocese of Cleveland,* Cleveland: M. R. M'Cabe, 1882.

Grünewald, J., *Die Rechtsverhältnisse an Kirchenstühlen,* Görres-Gesellschaft zur Pflege der Wissenschaft im katholischen Deutschland, Hefte 1-5, Köln: Verlag und Druck von T. P. Bachem, 1908; Heft 6- , Paderborn: Druck und Verlag von Ferdinand Schöningh, 1909- .

Guilday, Peter, *A History of the Councils of Baltimore (1791-1884),* New York: The Macmillan Co., 1932.

Guilfoyle, Merlin Joseph, *Custom,* The Catholic University of America Canon Law Studies, n. 105, Washington, D. C.: The Catholic University of America, 1937.

Guiniven, John Joseph, *The Precept of Hearing Mass,* The Catholic University of America Canon Law Studies, n. 158, Washington, D. C.: The Catholic University of America Press, 1942.

Gulczynski, John Theophilus, *The Desecration and Violation of Churches,* The Catholic University of America Canon Law Studies, n. 159, Washington, D. C.: The Catholic University of America Press, 1942.

Houck, George F., *A History of Catholicity in Northern Ohio and in the Diocese of Cleveland from 1749 to December 31, 1900,* 2 vols., Vol. II, Michael Carr, *Biographical,* Cleveland: Press of J. B. Savage, 1903.

Hynes, Michael J., *History of the Diocese of Cleveland, Origin and Growth (1847-1952)*, Diocese of Cleveland: World Publishing Company, 1953.

Kremer, Michael N., *Church Support in the United States,* The Catholic University of America Canon Law Studies, n. 61, Washington, D. C.: The Catholic University of America, 1930.

Lord, Robert H.-Sexton, John E.-Harrington, Edward T., *History of the Archdiocese of Boston in the Various Stages of Its Development, 1604-1943,* 3 vols., New York: Sheed & Ward, 1944.

McManus, Frederick Richard, *The Congregation of Sacred Rites,* The Catholic University of America Canon Law Studies, n. 352, Washington, D. C.: The Catholic University of America Press, 1954.

Michiels, Gommarus, *Normae Generales Juris Canonici,* editio altera, 2 vols., Tornaci: Typis Societatis S. Joannis Evangelistae, Desclée et Socii, 1949.

Nilles, Nicolaus, *Commentaria in Concilium Plenarium Baltimorense Tertium ex Praelectionibus Academicis Excerpta,* 2 vols. in 1, Oeniponte: Typis et Sumptibus Fel. Rauch (C. Pustet), Pars I, Editio Domestica, 1888; Pars II, 1890.

O'Brien, Kenneth R., *The Nature of Support of Diocesan Priests in the United States of America,* The Catholic University of America Canon Law Studies, n. 286, Washington, D. C.: The Catholic University of America Press, 1949.

Oppenheim, Philippus, *Institutiones Systematico-Historicae in Sacram Liturgiam,* Series I, 6 vols., Taurini: Marietti, 1937-1941.

Ramstein, *A Manual of Canon Law,* 2. ed., Hoboken, N. J.: Terminal Printing & Publishing Co., 1948.

Regatillo, Eduardus F., *Institutiones Iuris Canonici,* 5. ed., 2 vols., Santander: Editorial Sal Terrae, 1956.

Reiffenstuel, Anacletus, *Jus Canonicum Universum,* 5 vols. in 7, Parisiis, 1864–1882.

Ryder, Raymond A., *Simony,* The Catholic University of America Canon Law Studies, n. 65, Washington, D. C.: The Catholic University of America, 1931.

Shea, John Gilmary, *History of the Catholic Church in the United States,* 4 vols., New York, 1886-1892.

Smith, S. B., *Notes on the Second Plenary Council of Baltimore,* New York: P. O'Shea, 1874.

Spalding, J. L., *The Life of the Most Rev. M. J. Spalding, D.D., Archbishop of Baltimore,* New York: Christian Press Association Publishing Co. [no date given].

Thaner, F., *Die* SUMMA MAGISTRI ROLANDI BANDINELLI *nachmals Papstes Alexander III,* Innsbruck, 1874.

Van der Stappen, J. F., *Sacra Liturgia,* 3. ed., 5 vols., Mechliniae: H. Dessain, 1911-1915.

Vermeersch, A.-Creusen, I., *Epitome Iuris Canonici,* 3 vols., Vol. I, 7. ed., 1949; Vol. II, 7. ed., 1954, Mechliniae: H. Dessain.

Webster's New International Dictionary of the English Langauge, 2. ed., 3 vols., Springfield, Mass.: G. & C. Merriam Co., 1953.

Weninger, F. X., *Epitome Pastoralis ad Usum Cleri in Statibus Foederatis Americae,* Buffalone: Typis C. Wieckmann & S. Brandt, 1855.

Wernz, F. X.-Vidal, P., *Ius Canonicum ad Codicis Normam Exactum,* 7 vols. in 8, Vol. IV, Tom. I, *De Rebus,* Romae: Apud Aedes Universitatis Gregorianae, 1934.

Woywod, Stanislaus-Smith, Callistus, *A Practical Commentary on the Code of Canon Law,* 1. printing, revised and enlarged edition, of 2 vols. combined in 1, New York City: Joseph F. Wagner, Inc., 1952.

Ziolkowski, Thaddeus S., *The Consecration and Blessing of Churches,* The Catholic University of America Canon Law Studies, n. 187, Washington, D. C.: The Catholic University of America Press, 1943.

PERIODICALS

American Ecclesiastical Review, The; American Ecclesiastical Review, Vols. I-XXXII, Philadelphia, 1889-1905; *The Ecclesiastical Review,* Vols. XXXIII-CIX, Philadelphia, 1905-1943; *The American Ecclesiastical Review,* Vol. CX- , Washington, D. C., 1944- .

Homiletic and Pastoral Review, The; Homiletic Monthly and Catechist, Vols. I-XVII, New York, 1901-1917; *The Homiletic Monthly,* Vol. XVIII, New York, 1918; *The Homiletic Monthly and Pastoral Review,* Vols. XIX, XX, New York, 1918-1920; *The Homiletic and Pastoral Review,* Vol. XXI- , New York, 1920- .

Jurist, The, Washington, D. C., 1941- .

ALPHABETICAL INDEX

BIOGRAPHICAL NOTE

Albert Charles Ernst was born July 18, 1926, at Shreveport, Louisiana. At an early age he moved with his family to Pine Bluff, Arkansas, where he attended Annunciation Academy and Pine Bluff High School. Upon his graduation from high school, he entered the military service with the United States Naval Air Corps. In September, 1947, after attending the University of Redlands, Redlands, California, the University of California at Los Angeles, and Loyola University of the South, New Orleans, Louisiana, he entered St. John's Home Missions Seminary, Little Rock, Arkansas. The following year he was awarded the Degree of Bachelor of Arts from Little Rock College. On May 30, 1953, he was ordained to the Sacred Priesthood by the Most Reverend Albert L. Fletcher, D.D., Bishop of Little Rock. Shortly thereafter he was assigned as an assistant to St. Patrick's Parish, in the city of North Little Rock. In September, 1954, he was transferred to the Faculty of St. John's Home Missions Seminary, and, under the direction of his bishop, he enrolled in the Canon Law School of The Catholic University of America, Washington, D. C., from which he received the Baccalaureate Degree in Canon Law in June of 1955, and the Licentiate Degree in Canon Law in June of 1956.

CANON LAW STUDIES *

No. 375. Kelleher, Rev. Francis T., A.B., J.C.L., Judicial expenses.

No. 376. Bantigue, Rev. Pedro N., J.C.L., The Provincial Council of Manila of 1771.
(Its text followed by a commentary on *Actio II, De Episcopis*).

No. 377. Burns, Rev. Dennis J., J.C.L., Matrimonial indissolubility: contrary conditions.

No. 378. Deutsch, Rev. Bernard F., J.C.L., Jurisdiction of pastors in the external forum.

No. 379. Dunnivan, Rev. John P., A.B., J.C.L., Prejudicial attempts in pending litigation.

No. 380. Ernst, Rev. Albert C., A.B., J.C.L., Free admission to the church for sacred rites.

No. 381. Frattin, Peter Louis, J.C.L., The matrimonial impediment of impotence: occlusion of the spermatic ducts and vaginismus.

No. 382. Henry, Rev. Charles W., O.S.B., A.B., S.T.L., J.C.L., Canonical relations between bishops and abbots at the beginning of the tenth century.

No. 383. Hoffman, Rev. Lawrence J., A.B., S.T.B., J.C.L., Clergy Conferences: Canon 131.

No. 384. Markham, Rev. James J., A.B., S.T.L., J.C.L., The Sacred Congregation of Seminaries and Universities of Studies.

No. 385. McGrath, Rev. John J., A.B., LL.B., J.C.L., A comparative study of crime and its imputability in ecclesiastical criminal law and in American criminal law.

No. 386. McGuire, Rev. James D., O.R.S.A., J.C.L., The postulancy.

No. 387. Munday, Rev. James E., J.C.L., Ecclesiastical Property in Australia and New Zealand.

No. 388. Murphy, Rev. Joseph P., A.B., J.C.L., The laws of the State of New York affecting church property.

No. 389. Pickard, Rev. Wm. M., J.C.L., Judicial experts: a source of evidence in ecclesiastical trials.

No. 390. Ruddy, Rev. James, J.C.L., The Apostolic Constitution *Christus Dominus:* text, translation and commentary, with short annotations on the Motu Proprio *Sacram Communionem.*

No. 391. Vanyo, Rev. Leo V., A.B., J.C.L., Requisites of intention in the reception of the sacraments.

* For a complete list of the available numbers of this series apply to the Catholic University of America Press, 620 Michigan Avenue, N.E., Washington (17), D. C., for a general catalog.

www.ingramcontent.com/pod-product-compliance
Lightning Source LLC
LaVergne TN
LVHW050213080826
844660LV00012B/407

* 9 7 8 0 8 1 3 2 2 5 4 0 1 *